MANIFESTATION THRU VISUALIZATION & AFFIRMATION

Law of Attraction With Workbook

Linn Random

Chapters

Cover Artist: DesignerHala at FiverR.com
Editor: Paige Lawson

Release date: 07/20/2022

Dedication Page

To my son and his beautiful wife, Michael & Elisabeth.

And to the man who keeps who keeps
me grounded, Chris Belote.

CHAPTER 1 THE LAW OF ATTRACTION

We live in a Universe governed by invisible laws. We can't see them or touch them, but they are forever playing in the background of our lives. Without exception, these laws work equally for all and fall into two categories.

The first set of laws are physical. The physical laws govern our corporeal universe. The second group of laws are known as metaphysical laws.

The metaphysical laws govern our inner world and create and project our inner thoughts into the things that make up our physical world. Metaphysical laws reflect to us exactly what we think, speak and feel about ourselves.

We are more familiar with the physical laws of the universe. For instance, the Law of Gravity.

You can't see the Law of Gravity or touch it, but you know it's there. Everyone and everything responds to this law. Gravity binds us to this planet. Gravity keeps the tides on time, the stars in place and the solar system spinning.

You don't have to prompt the Law of Gravity to work, you simply have to let go, and any object you are holding will drop to the ground.

Another example of a physical law is the Law of Centrifugal Force. You cannot escape this law, for if you drive too fast around a curve, you will likely find your vehicle in the ditch.

These laws are impersonal and work for everyone. They do not reward or punish; they simply exist. Physical laws are impartial. The Law of Electricity works for both the surgeon the criminal who uses using electricity to steal.

We may not like the destructive powers of hurricanes, typhoons or tornados, but they keep the planet cool and life flourishing.

Electricity has always been available to us since we lived in caves, but it didn't come into our collective experience until we discovered the laws of electricity and how to use it. We are just now discovering how to access and tap into metaphysical laws such as the law of attraction.

Metaphysical laws are not new. Metaphysics were taught by scholars, priests and philosophers and can be traced back to the ancient mystery schools of Egypt and to the Druids.

Under starry skies, the Druids would chant, "As above, so below." The Druids understood the deep meaning and the powerful connection between the words "as above" (the mind), "so below" (the physical plane). This simple concept is as true today as when they were first spoken.

A little over a century ago, the New Thought movement was taught by the Theosophy societies and American Transcendentalists such as Ralph Waldo Emerson, Henry David Thoreau and their counterparts. As these ideas formed, they began to organize into religions such as my faith, Religious Science.

Ernest Holmes, the founder of the Church of Religious Science, was one of those New Thought leaders. He wrote *The Science of Mind,* which included the laws of attraction. His book offers insights and explanations on the conscious and subconscious mind and how we can control the physical world through this science.

In 2006, author Rhonda Byrne popularized the Law of Attraction through her book, *The Secret.* Today, you'll find hundreds of books, tapes, mediations and CDs on the Law of Attraction.

The Law of Attraction is perceived as magical alchemy. When incorporated into our lives, it will bring any desire from the etherical plane into our physical universe. However,

understanding how the Law of Attraction works is not quite as simple as repeating a few affirmations and expecting immediate results.

The secret to the Law of Attraction is in the details where other laws come into play.

For instance, the Law of Attraction works with other laws like the Law of Vibration, the Law of Cause and Effect and the Law of Correspondence. All these laws must come into alignment for your desire to work.

The Law of Correspondence works directly with your vibrational energy. The Law of Correspondence states you draw into your experience the corresponding image you hold in your mind.

Christ stated in KJV Matthew 18:19, "Again I say unto you, that if two of you shall agree on earth as touching anything that they shall ask, it shall be done for them of my Father which is in heaven."

Many faiths interrupt this to mean two or more people united in prayer. While, I believe that can be so, I believe that the two are actually the intellectual mind and emotional energy. For, it is only when your desire is united with your emotion's manifestation will occur.

Your thoughts, your words and your energy must be in alignment. For instance, you can intellectually desire wealth but feel you don't deserve it or are unworthy of it. No amount of prayer will bring it into your experience. The Universe, the energy of Life and manifestation, will always respond to the more powerful emotion.

Here's one of my favorite examples to illustrate this principle. The intellect says, "I won't eat a donut because I am on a diet." The emotions, on the other hand, cry out with deep primordial remembrance of the pleasure of eating a donut and scream "Donut!". The emotions win. The emotions always win.

If you want the Law of Attraction to work in your life, it's important to understand how the Law of Attraction works in conjunction with other laws. Laws like the Law of Vibration.

The Law of Vibration states everything in the universe has its own vibrational energy.

Rocks, trees, plants, while appear stationary, are actually vibrating. The energy of rocks is low and dense so while you and I cannot pick up visible movement, science has proven rocks, crystals, trees, mountains, and everything else in our universe is moving and vibrating at various frequencies. We, as human beings, along with our animal counterparts have a higher vibration.

Do you recall that iconic scene in the movie *Jurassic Park*, when the Tyrannous Rex's foot hit the ground, and inside the car with the children, the water in the glasses revibrated? It is the same with our words. It is the same with our thoughts. Our words also carry within each vowel and consonant a vibrational energy.

In Hinduism and many eastern religions, followers will say, "Om" to raise their vibrational levels when in prayer and meditation. "Om" is a Sanskrit word that translates to 'source' or 'supreme'. The "om" is chanted to evaluate our frequency and energy to align and connect with the Divine.

This vibrational energy works in conjunction with the Law of Correspondence. For instance, you aren't going to generate a million-dollar lottery win unless your energy or vibration is aligned to a million dollars. You will only draw into your experience what you believe to be true about yourself. Your conscious and subconscious mind will attract the corresponding image in the real world.

If you find it difficult to accept a compliment, you will not up your financial game.

The Law of Attraction will not work if it hits an internal roadblock. These roadblocks are feelings of unworthiness or the negative thoughts you hold about yourself.

Aristotle was a renowned Greek philosopher whose wisdom is still taught in universities today. He wrote, "we do not have knowledge of a thing until we have grasped its why, that is to say, its cause." He stated there are four primary causes he wrote about them in his book Metaphysics.

Aristotle, Jesus, and other religious and philosophical leaders all caught the law of cause and effect. A cause in the physical world is heavy snow in the winter; the result is spring flooding.

In the metaphysical world, you are the principal cause of everything in your life.

What you believe about yourself will be manifested in the physical world. We are co-creators with God and create our own experiences.

From Proverbs, 23:7, the Bible says, "As a man thinketh in his heart, so is he".

In his book, The Science of Mind, Ernest Holmes states, "Life is a mirror and will reflect back to the thinker what he thinks into it." Holmes goes into great detail as he offers an explanation as to how thoughts are things.

In addition to your thoughts, you should be mindful of the power in your words. This is especially true when invoking the power of "I am" in your life.

When Moses asked for the name of God, God answered, "I am who I am." KJV, Exodus 3:14. You invoke this power every time you say, "I am". When you say these words, you are, in effect, co-creating with God, the Universe. When you say, I am sick; I am poor; I am unlovable, you bring the effect into your experience. Instead, say, I am health, I am wealth, or my wealth grows; I am love, loving, loveable, I am worthy of love. As you change your thoughts and the words you speak of yourself, you change your outer world.

In later chapters, we will explore our powers of co-creation but before we do, let's clean out any negative thoughts, feelings or past experiences that may block your good and your desire.

CHAPTER 2
What is Holding You Back?

Before we get into the how-to of manifestation, it's important to explore and uncover anything holding you back.

In this chapter, we'll find the reasons that keep people from achieving their desires. This includes beliefs about money, feelings of unworthiness, opinions about the self or others and lastly, why affirmations don't work.

If you want good, love, and abundance, then fully focus on those ideals. The Universe will respond in accordance to your thoughts and feelings.

If you focus on fear, lack, and the negative, the Universe will not only respond in kind but will return these negative thoughts and feelings back to you; multiplied.

As shared earlier, metaphysical laws are impartial. They neither reward nor punish. They will simply respond to whatever you give our attention to.

There's an old song about how the rich get rich, and the poor get children. The rich get rich because they focus on wealth and enjoying the pleasures money can buy. The poor are worried about paying bills, surviving, grocery or medical bills, and focusing on lack. Both groups are reaping their corresponding experiences.

The Universe will give you exactly what you think about. Therefore, pay careful attention to your thoughts, desires and words. Proclaiming even in jest, you can't afford that new handbag will reap the corresponding effect.

In addition to the Laws of Attraction, Correspondence and the Law of Cause and Effect, I am going to add the Law of Circulation. The Law of Circulation demands continuous flow. If you block the flow anywhere in the cycle, you hinder the flow of good in your life. If you feel unworthy or undeserving, you block the circulation of financial flow.

If you feel uncomfortable accepting a gift or even a compliment, the core problem is not money; it's your feeling of unworthiness.

Beliefs about Money

Money, in and of itself, is neither good nor evil. It's simply the commodity we currently use to acquire goods and services. Centuries ago, we were exchanging beads and seashells.

Many of us have a love/fear relationship with money.

For me, this fear of money began as a child. In Sunday School, I learned that money was the source of all evil, and if I loved money, I would go to hell. Yikes, I didn't want to go to hell. I wanted to go to heaven! I was also frightened by monsters under my bed and noises outside my window.

As I grew, I realized monsters weren't real. There was no such thing as the boogeyman and the sound of scarping outside my window was a tree branch that needed trimming.

Yet, the concept that money was evil lingered in the dark recesses of my subconscious mind. The often-heard declarations compounded from my parents that I was unworthy. Over time, my beliefs about money and feelings of unworthiness assimilated in my psyche and blocked my path to financial abundance for many years.

It took me a long time to realize I was a beloved child of God, worthy of every good thing. It took countless books, tapes, and CDs, as well as a lot of internal dialogue, to eradicate those thoughts and feelings.

What are your thoughts and beliefs about money? Do you feel awkward about accepting money? How do you feel a knot in your stomach or guilt when you spent a small portion on yourself? Do you in any way feel hesitant about accepting money or asking for a raise?

To understand your relationship with money, take a dollar bill and hold it in your hand. Close your eyes, and allow yourself to explore the thoughts and feelings you have about money. Let the money speak to you and listen to your internal dialogue.

See yourself receiving money and then visualize yourself handing money to someone else. Is there a lump in your throat or a knot in your stomach? Does your body constrict? Does your heart skip a beat, or does your sacral chakra recoil?

A long time ago, when we lived in caves, we listened to our bodies. We were alert and instinctively aware of the danger. After all, our lives were dependent on our senses. During that time, we were keenly aware of changes in air pressure and hurried to shelter when we felt the atmospheric variations. Back then, we paid attention to strangers and watched their body signals to indicate whether they were a friend or intended harm. We listened and trusted our gut and our intuitive selves.

Today, in our modern world, we have forgotten to listen to our bodies and ignore the warnings they try to share with us. We ignore these warnings and worry about being politically correct. Your body will be delighted to have you listen to it and will happily provide you with the answers you seek.

What does your body tell you about money?

I want you to visualize yourself sitting at your kitchen table, paying a bill. Do you write your check out with joy and gratitude for the service you received? Or do you fearfully watch your balance grow smaller? Identify all physical and emotional experiences as you spend your money. Your body is a barometer of your intuitive self.

Your physical reactions are indicators of your core beliefs. Sometimes the simple act of identifying negative thoughts or emotions will help you root them out.

To break any money blockage in your life, give. Cultivate giving money away without feeling a lump in your throat. Practice receiving a compliment without saying more than thank you. If any restrictions occur, identify and release them until there is nothing left but gratitude. Practice until you feel the delight of the experience and the deep-seated knowingness that the money you just gave away will return to you.

When you pay for your meal, see that money flowing from you to the server, the restaurant owner, and the farmer who buys the seed. Feel the happiness of each interaction by every person in the monetary chain. Watch as your money moves to the bankers and businesses and to all the people who enjoy the happy benefit you set into motion. Feel the happiness of the employees who can make their house payment or buy toys and food for their children.

Monies freely and lovingly given will return to you, multiplied. Learn to give and accept money with gratitude.

Let go of any negative thoughts you have about money. Replace those thoughts with an attitude of gratitude by happily and joyfully accepting the funds, funds you are worthy to accept and experience.

Practice the act of gracious receiving. Be open to receiving money and learn how to say thank you. To say anything other than thank you is to dishonor the giver. Thank the giver, thank God, and bless the funds.

I have noticed that people who have difficulty accepting money also have difficulty accepting a compliment. If you feel uncomfortable when someone says something nice to you, don't have a knee jerk response that tells the person the dress is old or dismisses their compliment. When you dismiss a kind word or thought, you are disrespecting their opinion as you are also telling the Universe, you are not worthy of such kind words. Practice saying thank you until you can accept a compliment with grace.

Money needs to be kept in a constant state of flow. It's okay to add to your savings or hold onto it for a prosperous future; just don't hold onto it out of the fear that if you spend it, it won't return.

Live in the Laws of Attraction and Circulation, and money, love, and abundance will flow continuously in your life.

Say with me, "I now accept love, health, harmony, and financial abundance in my life. I enjoy the flow of financial abundance in my life. I give generously, and I pay my bills knowing money is continuously flowing into my life. I am worthy of every good thing. I am worthy of an unending stream of financial abundance. And So It Is."

Another belief that holds people back is Ego, but it's not what you think.

Ego

The word Ego comes from the Latin pronoun I. The Ego is the image we hold of ourselves. It's the sum total of who we think we are and sometimes gets blended with the perception of what others think of us.

When we use the words ego or egotistical, we generally think of those words as unflattering terms used to describe vain, boastful, self-absorbed, and opinionated people. We believe being called egotistical is unbecoming in other people and certainly in ourselves.

There is another ego side, for having too little an ego or no ego can be just as damaging and debilitating. This aspect of the ego says to the self, "I am unworthy. I do not deserve good, love, or success." If the ego feels these statements are true, I can assure you of a sad life with poor outcomes.

For many of us, low opinions of ourselves began in childhood when critical words were spoken to us by parents, teachers, or schoolyard bullies or perhaps simply materialized in the dark shadows of our self-talk.

Feelings of unworthiness are as familiar to us as the lyrics of an old song that continuously plays in the background of our minds. Left unchecked, these long-standing melodies permeate every aspect of our lives. Feeling as though we're unworthy will keep us from our success. It will keep us from experiencing unlimited abundance, joy, good health and even love.

Words only hurt you if you believe they are true. You will never achieve success until you know you are worthy of every good thing.

Feeling everyone is worthy of success but you will keep you trapped in a chasm of unhappiness. Your choice is to remain in this dark pit of false narratives or rise from a distorted view of who you truly are.

You are special, perfect, whole, and complete. Read that sentence again and as you slowly digest each word, pause and internalize them and feel them in every cell of your body, for this is who you really are. You are special. You are perfect just as you are. You are whole and complete.

Everyone should have a healthy opinion of the self that is balanced, independent, and free from the opinions of others.

Now would be a good time to write down your thoughts and feelings about success.

A sales axiom states two reasons for doing anything: the real reason and the one that sounds good.

Your fear-born, false sense of ego may be telling you that you will never be able to leave your dead-end job or enjoy a lifestyle that others celebrate. In this instance, you rationalize that you are a good parent, partner, citizen staying in the job because it is the responsible thing to do. Is your answer the real reason or the one that sounds good? If the real reason is wrapped in feelings of unworthiness because you deserve nothing more than the dead-end job, check your unworthiness at the door and find a way to make your dreams happen.

Once you acknowledge and uncover the real reason for staying in an unhappy job, you will move forward in your life.

The belief that you're not worthy is a lie. To rise above feelings of unworthiness, you must raise your self-esteem.

Affirmations are wonderful, but you must believe your affirmations are true.

To change your opinion of yourself, begin by writing down a list of attributes you like about yourself. This is your starting place.

Write down and appreciate the good, strong, kind qualities you possess. When I began this exercise for myself, I could only conceive of one good thing about myself. It took days and weeks before I could add to my list, but I saw the good qualities within me as I did. I wasn't an ugly, victimized duckling after all. In time, I found a swan starring back at me from the mirror. The good qualities were always there; I had such a low opinion of myself, it took me a while to find them.

Keep working on your list; fill up page after page as you acknowledge and understand who you truly are. Review your list and add to it every day. This is your mission until you understand who you really are. As your list grows, so will your self-esteem, pride, and perception of the beautiful person you are.

Love and appreciate yourself every day; make it your mission to do at least one nice thing for yourself every day. Make you the star of your own life!

Do things you love. Doing things, you love honors yourself and your beautiful spirit. Action validates your internal dialogue that you are worthy. As you do things that nurture you by the sheer act of expressing love to yourself, you will come to believe it and realize the truth of who you really are. These small things grow into self-worth.

Make a date with yourself to enjoy a walk, read a book or do anything that uplifts you. Do whatever do need to do to make yourself feel special because you are.

You have always known you are special, now is the time to experience it by celebrating you.

Say I am worthy every minute of every day until you know it to be true. I can absolutely assure you will uncover a higher version of yourself, one who deserves every aspect of success.

Live in a no-judgment zone. Stop judging others for your judgment of others will eventually return on you. Judgment and unforgiveness for past mistakes and negative self-talk bind you and hamper movement and flow in your life. Live in a no-judgment zone. The shackles you bind yourself with will fall by the wayside. Living in a no-judgment zone will be freeing, and you will feel lighter.

And, regarding past regrets, keep in mind, you did the best always. So, as you would forgive a friend, forgive and let go of any past actions that hold you down. They are no part of your experience today. In fact, because of those events, you have become the beautiful person you are in the present.

Come to understand fully, your role in your life is not to play the victim but the star.

Focus on what makes you feel good and on that which enhances your experience. You will only experience financial abundance when you internalize and truly accept it.

As you uplift your sense of self, you will experience positive changes in your world. Raise your thoughts, emotions, and vibrations; you will create a new life for yourself with a healthy, balanced ego.

Spend some time writing down the good you do and how you have helped others. Write down your accomplishments, affirmations, and the dreams you have already fulfilled. See yourself as I see you. Someone who deserves and is worthy of success.

Your manifest destiny is to experience life and live with abundance with all good things.

In your meditation and visualization work, see yourself achieving your goal. Believe your dream is achievable. Your once upon a time is here and is now.

God will never give you a dream without fulfillment. Heaven wants you to succeed and be successful.

When Don't Affirmations Work?

An affirmation is a proclamation, a truth you claim to affect your life. Positive affirmations can shift consciousness and bring about a positive change in their physical world.

However, merely repeating a phrase or affirmation over and over again without investing energy into the words is merely wishful thinking.

I want you to think of your affirmation as a jet airplane.

Picture with me a beautiful, gleaming airplane sitting on the tarmac. You're in the captain's chair, but until you engage the engines, the jet is going to sit idling on the runway. By physically pushing the throttle forward, the engines roar to life and drive the plane forward before ascending into the powder-blue sky. It is the energy behind your words that will give your affirmations flight.

The first step is to believe your words. Breathe life into them. Feel their energy bubble up inside you. Belief combined with your emotional energy is truly the wind beneath your wings.

As stated before, when emotions and the intellect come into conflict, the emotions will always win. As previously stated, the Universe will always respond to the stronger call.

What you think about and dwell on, you will experience in the manifest plane. The Universe is always listening to what you say and what you feel.

Years ago, I would spend the first thirty minutes of each morning in prayer and meditation as I spiritually built my financial wealth. I truly sparked the Divine within me during my prayers and d , and I was one with my good. Oh, if only I could have stayed in those precious moments of oneness with my financial dreams!

You see, immediately after my morning meditations, I would check my bank balance and then spend the next twenty-three-plus hours worrying about money and what I perceived was my lack of it.

I set the Universal Laws of Attraction and Correspondence into play, which returned to me as an unending cycle of financial challenges.

Whatever we send out comes back multiplied.

As I grew in faith, I stopped that defeating cycle by turning my attention and completely focusing on abundance throughout the day. As I directed my attention and my thoughts to prosperity, the Universe opened the floodgates of financial increase as I lived in a prosperity consciousness.

What are you focusing your attention on throughout the day?

One of my favorite stories was heard at a Christian Science Lecture. My apologies to the speaker, whose name has become lost in time, but the picture he painted still resonates with me today.

He shared a story of an old lady who barely had enough to eat. Her children had deserted her, her husband had left her for another woman, and her home was falling apart. Lamenting her life, she went to her minister for solace.

"What have you asked God for?" the minister asked softly.

With tears in her eyes, she said in a voice barely above a whisper, "All I have ever asked God for was the crust of bread and a roof over my head."

The moral of this tale seems harsh, but the lesson is clear, each of us gets exactly what we ask for. Therefore, take care of what you are asking of Heaven.

A century ago, there is the story of an Irish lad who measured out a few loaves of bread and cheese for his long voyage across the Atlantic to America. He kept a close eye on his rations, but the bread grew moldy as the days passed, and the cheese went bad. Throughout the journey, he listened to the happy mealtimes shared by the other passengers. It wasn't until they neared the shore that he realized that his ticket included the daily meals. Your "ticket" to this life includes abundant.

In the KJV of the Bible, John 10:10, Jesus states, "I am come that they might have life, and that they might have it more abundantly."

Too often, we limit ourselves with false and self-limiting thoughts. How many of us ask for little when the Universe is willing to give us so much more if only we'd accept it? You were born to be successful. You were born success-filled. It's your nature.

If you are struggling to find abundance in your life, start by counting your blessings. Every morning, every night, thank God for your good. Walk through your home and touch and bless every piece of furniture, every article of clothing, the dishes you use and your refrigerator that stores your food. Make a list of your blessings and as your list grows, so will your attitude of gratitude and your finances.

Rise above fear and doubt through the knowingness that your affirmations and words are true. Energize those affirmations with the confidence found in your emotions.

I will often prescribe an affirmation when working with my clients, just as physicians give patients a prescription. Instead of two pills a day, I'd suggest they repeat an affirmation every hour on the hour.

Spend time daily in positive thoughts of prosperity, abundance, health and love.

Another reason why you don't achieve your desired outcome is due to outlining.

Outlining

Outlining is telling God exactly how your desire it to come about. This is called outlining. When you are too specific, you can sometimes block the very good you seek.

Another big reason you should not outline is that your vision may fall short of what the Universe had planned for you.

One of my clients wanted a new car. She came to me with her desire and then explained how this would occur in her life.

Her plan began with visiting a car dealership, test-driving the vehicle, and being offered payments she could afford, well, barely afford. I listened to her, and instead of outlining exactly how a new car would manifest, I recommended she start with the answer, the car she desired. She stopped outlining and focused on the car only. Three weeks later, her aunt called her. Her aunt could no longer drive and wanted to gift her with the exact car she had held in her visualization.

Don't outline; visualize your desired outcome. Start with the answer. Trust the Universe to deliver that which you desire.

Another example of outlining is a treasure map created

by someone hoping to attach a loving partner. These maps are filled with beautiful pictures of how and where to meet Mr. or Ms. Right, followed by a fairytale romance with the outcome of a lovely wedding. Treasure mapping can be fun, but take care about being too specific. For instance, you may romanticize an enchanted encounter while on vacation and fail to notice the guy who rides the elevator in your office building every day.

Treasure mapping can be fun but be open to all possibilities. I prefer you start with the answer and let the Universe do the heavy lifting.

I always recommend adding the phrase to any prayer or affirmation, "This or something better now manifests for me." This allows the Universe to give you something more than you can imagine.

Say your affirmation with belief, conviction, and focus on the outcome of your desire. Don't outline your desire, be open to the magic the Universe has in store for you.

If you put positive energy behind your affirmations and then release them to the Universe in peace and confidence, I assure you, the Universe will respond.

Hate

Hate is an enormous block and will effectively stop any good thing from coming into your life and impact your health and finances. Hate permeates into every nook and cranny of your life and spills into the lives around you.

Negative feelings about yourself or others will stop your dreams dead in their tracks. Hate creates a monumental blockage of huge proportions.

Hate, unforgiveness or negative thoughts and feelings about yourself or others block all good and damns the flow of abundance in your life.

Hating or holding a prejudice to any group, race, religion, or sexual orientation will obstruct your good.

Once when working with a client, we examined her

thoughts and judgments about others in her life. She felt she led a charmed life, well, except for the neighbor who held different political views than her own. She was venomous in her hatred of the political signs in her neighbor's yard and hated the candidate. As we talked about her neighbor, she realized hating that one person was keeping her from her desired good. In the end, she concluded that hating her neighbor and or the candidate was not worth it.

When she released her anger, she felt peace. Serenity filled her home, and the good she longed for began to arrive. Coincidently, her neighbor, without any prompting, removed the signs in her yard.

Hate blocks the law of circulation and spills over into every area of your life. Hating a single person, past or present, creates an imbalance. Hate blocks the free flow of love and good in your life. Hatred blocks the Law of Attraction.

Release any negative emotions that block you from experiencing your good. Live in a no judgment zone.

You can only feel one of two emotions at any given time. Those feelings are either love or fear. Fear manifests itself as hate, anger and negative emotion.

Let go of fear, let go of anger, let go of regret and let love be the foundation of having a healthier, happier and wealthier life.

Cord Cutting

On occasion, there seems to be something elusive holding us back from our success.

We may not be cognizant of the cause, but we know we are experiencing the effect. The causation eludes us.

If so, it may be a lingering Etherical Cord that binds us to a forgotten experience in our current life or perhaps a past life.

I see etherical cords as thin, fine, shimmering, silvery, magical tubing that glitters and sparkles between us and those we love. While most cannot see these etherical cords, we can feel them binding us to those we love and those who love us. We can feel them tug at us when we sense a loved one is in distress or even danger.

These cords also bind us to experiences, places, and things.

Etherical cords connect us to loved ones and strangers with whom we feel an instant connection. We are so immediately familiar with these strangers; it seems as if we have known them all our lives. There is never a moment of awkwardness with these new friends, and even the silence seems natural.

The French term déjà vu means "already seen." Etherical Cords are déjà vu experiences that are also felt.

Etherical Cords can bind us to painful experiences, hurtful relationships, and traumatic events. Like soldiers with PTSD, an intrusive sound can take us back to those painful memories. Sometimes those memories can be from our current life or centuries past.

Have you ever met anyone who is inherently afraid of water, fire, or heights, with no experience in this lifetime to base it upon? These fears and frightening memories may not have come from a childhood event but from another life lived centuries ago.

Sometimes the frightening visions you conjure in your dreams are not nightmares or a product of an overactive imagination; they are memories.

Whether in this lifetime or a previous lifetime, we may hold on to buried memories or experiences that are so deep, we can no longer recall the trauma. Still, the etherical cord and the effect will remain until we release these harrowing events.

Once when I was working with a beautiful young woman, I could sense a past relationship was holding her back from experiencing the love she now longed for. I could sense she was still bound by the strong etherical cord she had created between her abusive lover and the memories she held of him.

"Do you think of him more than three times a week?" I asked.

She laughed. "I think of him three times an hour."

She was tied to a relationship that had ended years ago. The painful relationship was keeping her from experiencing a loving relationship she now craved.

By identifying this unhealthy cord, we began working on cutting this unhealthy fetter. It took several cord cuttings to sever this particular tie completely. While we worked on this, she also learned to reprogram her energy to attract a loving partner who would treat her with love and respect. It took several weeks, but in the end, she was successful. As if on cue, a man who seemed to be everything she had dreamed about came into her life. Today, she is living happily ever after with a new husband, who treasures her and supports her every dream.

Some Etherical Cords are not so easily identifiable. For instance, we may have spoken vows of poverty in a past life when we were monks, priests, or in a holy order. I made such a vow of poverty in the eleventh century and brought it forward with me to this lifetime. I had to cut those vows before I could create a new experience of financial good in my life.

If any of these words or experiences resonate within you, a cord may need to be cut. You don't need to remember the moment you made such a vow or revisit a past life. It's simply enough to know it's there.

The act of cutting a cord does not have to be a complicated

ceremony. In fact, it's very simple.

I work with Archangels, so when I need to cord cut, I call on Archangel Michael and ask him to use his fiery sword to sever my ties to any person, place, or thing that does not serve me. After a cord-cutting, I always ask Archangel Raphael to salve the wound with his green healing light to complete the healing.

For some etherical cords, a single cord-cutting will do. Other cords are strong and will regrow. If this is the case, be aware that some need to be cut several times before they completely dissipate. Cut cords until you are no longer bound to people or painful memories that haunt you. They have no place in your current life.

There are many different methods for cord-cutting. Find one that feels right and natural to you.

If you feel you need to contact a professional, some wonderful metaphysical practitioners can assist you in cord cutting on the internet.

Keep the loving, beautiful cords that bind you to loving relationships, but cut any cords that bind you or keep you from experiencing your good.

Every day, I urge you to meditate, to connect with the Universe and elevate your consciousness. Look at things, beliefs you hold that are keeping you from achieving your success. Every day, I urge you to spend time in meditation and visualization.

You were born to succeed; you have within you the ability to make the magic happen. It's your birthright.

In the next chapter, I will show you how to fast-track that which you desire with Heaven's fire.

CHAPTER 3 VISUALIZATION - HEAVEN'S FIRE

Visualization is the technique of creating a visual image in your mind. I truly believe it is one of the keystones of activating the Law of Attraction in our lives.

When we use visualization and add the power of emotional energy into our focused intention, we ignite the fire of heaven to the image of that which we desire.

What we think or dwell upon comes into our experience. When we visualize our desire, it signals the Universe to bring into our vision into the manifest plane.

The subconscious mind accepts your imagery as real.

Our bodies respond to visual or audio stimuli from our subconsciousness. For instance, if I ask you to visualize the warm, fresh, sweet scent of freshly baked bread or apple pie and like Pavlov's dog, you will begin to salivate. You have this reaction because your mind doesn't understand the difference between real and not real.

If you are familiar with the taste of an apple, your body receives the cues and memory, and your body will respond whether the pie is real or imagined. Similarly, if I ask you to imagine the tart taste of fresh lemon, you might pucker at the thought of the lemon's tartness.

Daydreams are not targeted visualizations. Daydreams are whimsical thoughts that float like fluffy white clouds across our minds. They have no real direction and are unable to latch onto anything tangible because they lack substance. Our daydreams are only in our psyches for a few moments before they fade away. Daydreams are mini-fantasies that give your mind a momentary mental break from the daily routines and activities.

On rare occasions, daydreams can produce results, but only if enough energy is put into them.

Physical therapists have long shared that patients who imagine walking or moving achieve faster results than those who do not. In fact, visualizations have been a well-documented method for improving health, increasing physical endurance, and healing injuries.

There are sports superstars, modern-day Olympians and athletes worldwide who use visualization to improve their physical performance.

To bring your desire into the physical plane, have a clear picture in your mind of your desire. Start with the answer.

For a moment, let's suggest you want to manifest a new car. First, write or state your intention with energy behind each word. Align with the energy of owning the car of your dreams and put emotional energy into your visualization.

Give thanks as you imagine driving your new car and the pride of ownership. Always end your visualization of affirmation. This or something better now manifests for me.

When it was time for me to purchase a new car, I printed a picture of a Nissen Rogue and had it framed on my desk.

I spent time visualizing my Rogue in the morning and before bed.

But I also added waking thoughts and images, and emotions when I was driving to and from work or out on an errand. I used that time to infuse my emotional energy into car ownership. When I'd see a Nissen Rogue, I'd think that's what my car looks like. When I saw my vehicle in a store window, I'd reimagine the image with that of a Nissen Rogue. At red lights, I'd say my simple affirmation, "Thank you Father Mother God, for my new Nissen."

Align your energy with the pleasure of owning a new car. Feel, truly feel and internalize how wonderful your new car is to drive. Imagine your fingers wrapped around the new steering wheel. Imagine how easily it will take a turn and how smooth as it glides to a safe stop. Envisage how the new seats will feel, the elegant dashboard shines, or how easy it is to park and handle. Image how your new car will sound when you click the automatic lock or how pretty it will look in your driveway or parking spot.

Every time I thought of my new car, I gave thanks and allowed an overwhelming sense of gratitude to bubble up within me until I felt the excitement of owning the Nissen. I'd conclude by affirming, "this or something better was coming into my life".

I never gave thought to how my new car was going to come into my experience. I just went through the visualization and manifest process. And within the next month, the exact car was in my driveway with payments I could easily afford.

Throughout the day, connect to your visualization through act, in word and action.

Please note, when doing any manifestation or visualization, follow the Universal principle of do no harm. If your visualization involves how you are doing to steal, cheat or involve yourself in an adulterous affair, you will find yourself in the middle of bad karma. Do no harm.

Live your life as if your visualization was already true, and it will manifest in your life faster than you could ever imagine.

End with your Visualization by saying, "This or something better now manifests in my life," and say, "Amen" or "And So It is!"

As you move through the chapters of this book, you will find visualizations you can use, adapt or create your own.

Make your visualization as real as possible. This includes adding the five senses into your imagery. The five senses are sight, sound, smell, taste, and touch.

As a mystery and romantic suspense author, I add in as many of the five senses to each scene as possible. If my heroine is walking down the stairs, I'll have her touch the banister and write something like, she traced her fingertips across the top of the railing, momentarily distracted by the smooth, cool texture of the wood.

I want you to do the same with your visualization. In each image in your meditation, use your five senses. For instance, if you are visualizing yourself at the beach, take a moment to imagine the fresh scent of salty air, listen to the screech of seagulls as they glide atop the waves, feel the grittiness of the sand below your feet or feel the soft brush of a wisp of hair as it is blown across your cheek.

You breathe life into your imagery by adding in the five senses, sight, sound, smell, taste, and touch. The more real you make this imagery, the deeper you connect with it, the faster your mind will embrace your image, and the faster the Universe will respond to it.

What follows is my general guide to visualization. The more you infuse emotional energy into the details, the faster your dreams will come true.

General Visualization Guidelines

1. Have a clear picture in your mind of your Desire.
2. State your Intention with Energy behind each word.
3. Prepare yourself by Grounding, Meditation, and Connecting to the Universe.
4. Align your emotional energy with that that your
5. Visualize your Desired Outcome with heartfelt passion, emotional energ and feeling into your Imagery. Infuse Love, detail into every aspect of your Visualization. Add in your sensory compo nents to your imagery.
6. End your Visualization with an overwhelming sense of Gratitude and say This or something better now manifests for me.
7. Release your Desire to the Universe in peace, knowing the Universe will

8.   Close your visualization by saying, "Amen" or "And So It is!"

Throughout the day, connect to your Visualization through act, in word and action. With a dedicated knowingness, your Desire is already true.

Write an easy to say affirmation and say it every hour on the
an hour or at select times throughout the day.

Live as though your Vision is true, and the here are now, will manifest into your life.

Chapter 4 The Process of Manifestation

Before you start the manifestation process, I recommend you have a clear vision of your desired outcome.

If your goal is to drive cross country from New York to Hollywood, you'd prepare a road map from your location to Tinsel Town. Without a map or GPS to help guide you, you could find yourself anywhere between Seattle to the Mexican border.

Likewise, you should begin with a clear understanding of what you truly desire in the manifest process. I have worked with many clients who have stated they wanted to manifest more money, but in actuality, my clients realized they did not want more money, but they wanted a home, or their student loan paid or the feeling of security that money represented. Be clear and specific in your desire.

There is nothing wrong with having a prosperity mindset. After all, abundance is your birthright. Being specific ramps up the manifestation process and brings your exact desire into the physical plane.

I have noticed that many people get lost in the manifestation process by not understanding the importance of the 'now'. They live their lives in a continuous loop of past memories, past lovers, past mistakes, or they spent too much time in the future worrying about what may or may not happen. We affect the future through our present consciousness. We affect our future by living in the now.

By focusing on the now, we manifest our dreams. By aligning our consciousness with that which we desire, we perfectly manifest our dreams.

The Energy of Alignment

To manifest a million-dollar paycheck, you first need to align yourself with abundance, affluence and prosperity.

Let's take a look at the guy across town who brought a winning lottery ticket. You may have read about him. He lived in the trailer with no heat or air conditioner in his home. You would not have taken him for a millionaire by the clothes her wore. However, internally, he had aligned himself with a million-dollar lottery win. Not only did he see himself as a lottery winner, but he also knew how to release to the Universe. The Universe simply responded to this energy and made sure he was in line to buy a winning ticket.

He didn't outline how he would achieve this dream; he simply visualized winning and internalized a successful outcome. Whether he was aware of it or not, he was perfectly following the steps of manifestation.

1. Energy Alignment
2. Visualization infused with emotional energy.
3. An attitude of gratitude and joy
4. Release to the Universe.

So many of us fail to manifest because we get in our own way. Let's look at the manifestation process and understand where he succeeded and where we failed.

1. Energy Alignment. We feel unworthy to accept our desire. We are too busy focusing on lack and not truly accepting our ability to win a million dollars.

2. Visualization infused with emotion-we put no joy into our desire, we held no belief that we were capable of winning, we put not angel fire into our dream. We didn't see holding the winning ticket in our hands and the delight when we realized we had won.

3. Attitude of gratitude-we failed to be grateful for what we have, and we failed to appreciate our good. We believed others are deserving of such a win, but not us.   4. Failure to release to God, the Universe-we didn't 'let go' of our beliefs, in our lack, we indulged in a type of self-pity, holding onto our victimhood and never released in love, joy peace with the knowledge and assurance that we won.

Once, when I was working on manifesting a child, I saw the prettiest little carrousel in a shop window. The price was $25.00, an amount I thought was a frivolous expenditure, but I loved it. I could see it sitting in my future child's bedroom.

It was July in Florida, and it was hot, Florida hot. After I returned home, I thought about the carrousel and fell asleep daydreaming of the carrousel in my future baby's nursery. A short time later, I woke to hear the phone ringing.

As we were clearing our land, the previous winter, we put an ad in the newspaper to sell wood for $25.00 a pick-up load. As I mentioned, it was now the middle of summer and the small three-line classified had long come and gone. My husband and I had forgotten it.

That midsummer day, I woke to the persistent ringing of the phone. There was a man on the other line who asked if we still had wood to sell. As we had a bit leftover, he came and picked a load of firewood to which he happily paid $25.00, the exact amount of the carrousel.

I never did get the carrousel, though I did manifest a son against all the doctors' prognosis. However, it was the lesson in manifestation that I never forgot.

When I laid down for a nap that day, I had no thought of how I would obtain an extra $25. I simply visualized the outcome. The joy I felt of how lovely the carrousel would look in the nursery lulled me into a quiet sleep. I didn't put any restrictions on how the $25 would come about. I simply saw the carrousel resting on a table. I started with the answer and fell into a serene peace seeing it in my son's room. I released the images to the Universe, and the Universe set about to make my desire come true.

Across town that same afternoon, the old man who brought the firewood said he found the community paper among some old magazines he was going to throw away. Our ad jumped out at him. Even though it was in the middle of summer, he was prompted to call us. It's still a marvel and a miracle how all this happened, but this is exactly how manifestation works. I had aligned my consciousness with the end result, and the Universe brought me the funds to make it happen.

The Universe and God support us when we align ourselves to what we desire, infuse our energy with passion, and then give thanks before releasing it to the Universe. The Universe will bring our manifestation into our reality.

If you feel unworthy of your desire, the Universe will support that. The Universe is impartial and will simply bring into your experience that you think about and focus upon. It does not reward or punish. It will give you that which you align your thoughts, words and feelings to. That which you send out comes back multiplied.

I can assure you; God will never give you a dream without also giving you the answer or solution. God, the Universe, works with you as co-creator of your world.

If you desire a home, align yourself with home ownership, and your home will manifest exactly to the value you feel you are worthy of and aligned to. If you cannot fully embrace a nice suburban home or a condo on the beach, you won't manifest it.   Before you can fill a bicycle tire with air, you first have to draw air into the hand pump before starting to fill the tire. The same is true when drawing water from a well. Before you can draw the well-water, you first have to prime the pump. It is the same with energy.

Infuse the energy within you with the pure emotional excitement of manifesting your desire. Create a feeling of euphoria inside you by completely embracing the joy of possessing that which you desire. This is the magic of emotion.

Your energy is the powerhouse that brings your desire into the manifest plane.

If you want a car or a home, when you allow the exultation to bubble up inside you, the feeling of owning that car or walking through your new home. The powerful energy within you is the fire of heaven that ignites the manifestation process within you.

If you desire a companion, fill yourself with love. Allow the emotional energy of love to bubble up from inside you until your heart feels like it will burst from its joy. Become one with the emotional energy of love, and the Universe will move mountains to bring your dream to your feet.

Let's walk through this exercise by manifesting a diamond necklace. First, let go of any negative thinking, such as never owning something so lovely or I don't have the money for such an extravagance.

Please note, and I want to stress, I am absolutely not permitting you to put this necklace on your credit card, which will only bring regret and worry. This exercise is through the manifestation process only.

So, in this example, let's align ourselves with the necklace. Start with the answer as I did my little carrousel.

State your intention. "I now manifest a diamond necklace."

Now imagine how it will look on you. How will it feel to wear it? Does it feel heavy or light? Notice how it sparkles around your neck. How does it feel smooth, or are you aware of the well-defined edges? Imagine your friends and strangers telling you how beautiful it looks on you. See yourself accepting their compliments. Put as much feeling and imagery into this visualization as possible.

Close your visualization with an attitude of gratitude. I say, "Thank you, Father-Mother-God, for my lovely necklace. This or something better now manifests in my life." and then, release your visualization to the Universe knowing, secure in the knowledge, the Universe will manifest that necklace. Then move on, let go, with the knowledge you have put your manifestation into the desire of a diamond necklace.

This mini-exercise was about a necklace, but it could be about anything you want to manifest.

The Universe does not know big or small. It only knows what is. The Universe will respond by manifesting that which you wish to co-create with it. You can as easily create a house, a companion, money in the bank or, as I did, a beautiful son.

Align your consciousness and subconscious with your emotional energy and connect it with your dream.

The last step in the manifestation process is release. Let go and let the Universe bring your desire from the ether into the manifest world.

Think positive thoughts 24/7 about your desire, keep your energy focuses on a positive outcome and know it will be true in your life. Speak with your power positively.

Your happily ever after is here and now only if you know it to be true.

Let's look now at the incredible power of the words "I am." I mentioned this before, but I want to dive deeper into the true power of the words, "I am."

The Power of I Am

As thoughts are things but so, are words. Take care with what you think and say especially when you invoke the almighty power of God, which you do every time you say the words "I am".

When Moses asked God, what was God's name, God replied, Exodus 3:14, KJV, "And God said unto Moses, I am that I am: and he said, thus shalt thou say unto the children of Israel, I am hath sent me unto you."

When I was a child, I thought the name 'I am" was a strange name for God. As I grew in my faith, I came to understand that every time I said the words "I am", I was invoking the power of God within me.

We are the co-creators with God. We, in effect, have the

same rights, privileges, healing and manifestation powers of Jesus. And when we speak with authority, we can expect to see results.

In Matthew 14:14-21, Jesus took five loaves, and the two fishes, looked up to heaven, blessed the food and divided it among his disciples. When they were done, they found twelve baskets of loaves and fishes leftover. Does this mean you can turn water into wine? Walk on water? Bring back the dead? I would say yes, but only if you believed you could.

Jesus was able to perform these miracles because He understood the law. He believed His word would be answered, and He manifested the result.

People around the world practice the act of Firewalking. Firewalking is the ability to walk barefoot across a bed of hot embers or stones without burning the feet. This practice dates back to 1200 BC. You may wonder how or even why people would want to do such a thing. They do it to achieve the manifest ability to do so.

When you speak your word, you are invoking your God-power, cocreator with the universe. When you say, I am sick, I am poor, I am having relationship troubles, the Universe, God, hears you and will mirror your inner world with your outer world.

If you say or think, I am poor; you will be. If you say, no one will ever love me or I am unworthy, you will be challenged to find your person. Say or think about food, a moment on the lips, a lifetime on the hips, and the Universe will make it so. Don't say even in jest that you have more bills at the end of the month, for the Universe is listening and will make it so. Watch your words.

Pay close attention to your thoughts, your energy and your feelings.

Whatever you say or think will return and sometimes return multiplied. It says so in the Bible. Galatians 6:7-9, KJV, "Be not deceived; God is not mocked: for whatsoever a man soweth, that shall he also reap."

Don't think you will get away with any self-defeating or

negative thoughts for whatever you think of, focus on, say, will be manifested in your life. It's the cause before the effect. It's how the law of karma works in your life.

Therefore, take care and pay close attraction to what you say and what you think. Be knowledgeable when you say, I am, for you are invoking the power of God.

The Power of Now

Once as an early metaphysical practitioner of my faith, I found myself sick in bed with a fever. I was doing my prayer work, but as the days passed, I remained ill.

I finally called my spiritual practitioner and asked: "What am I doing wrong?"

"Tell me your affirmation," she said. To which I responded, "I'll be better tomorrow." As soon as I heard my own response, I heard the answer, and I laughed.

The Universe was responding perfectly to me. I realized tomorrow was, like the song, only a day away. So, I changed my affirmation to "I am better Now."

By living in the now, the Universe responded to my affirmation, and the next day, I woke, restored to health.

If you have not read it, I recommend Eckhart Tolle's book, *The Power of Now: A Guide to Spiritual Enlightenment.* Eckart Tolle explained in his beautiful book how to live in the present.

To help you understand the now, I want to share I am an Akashic Record Reader. The Akashic Records is the repository of our every thought, word, deed, feeling, and energy behind our feelings and emotions. They are the storehouse of all information for every individual who has ever lived upon the earth. Each of us has our own personal Akashic Records, which is also known as the Book of Life. The Akashic Records are also known as God's Book of Remembrance.

References of the Akashic Records or the Book of Life are found in both the New and Old Testaments. You can find out more information about the Akashic Records in my book on

Reincarnation, Journey of the Soul.

To help you understand the now and that all time exists now, I ask you to envision a massive multiplex movie complex where all the shows are about you and are accessible at all times. The first theater could be a film of your toddler years, in the next a movie you could find a showing of your preteen years followed by a screening of the following years of your life. All movies are playing concurrently. You choose which movie or time; you want to view or experience.

Another example of how the Akashic Records can be found in the scroll bar on a YouTube video or a Netflix film. On the screen, you will find a scrubber or scrub bar.

You click on the play icon to view the video. When you hit the pause, the video will stop. To reengage, you click resume, and your video will move forward. If you want to fast forward, you simply drag the scroll to the end of the scrub bar.

The ball on the scrubber indicates where you are at the present moment. It's the now. You control the icon to move ahead or move back.

This is the same when you access the Akashic Records. You can view your past, present or see your future life.

Too many people are absorbed by the past and miss the present joys each day has to offer. They allow past memories to rob them of the present. Others are frozen in the grip of future events as they worry about what could or could not happen.

For me, living in the moment was something I had to cultivate. For many years, I struggled to let go of my thoughts of the past, or when not living there, I projected into the future and worried about unlimited possibilities. I was so lost in the past or future, I missed the "now".

When I got around to living in the present, I found peace, harmony and joy.

Stop and smell the roses is more than a song; it's about noticing the beauty around you, now.

Where do you spend your time? The past, the present or the future.

Anyone who knows me knows I love dogs. No creature on earth exemplifies living in the now quite like a dog. They don't carry grudges. They forgot you yelled at them the day before or were gone for hours. They are simply alive at the moment when you return home. Nothing matters to our dogs but the now. Dogs are just happy in the moment, in the now.

Understanding that all time is now and living in the now is empowering and galvanizing as you create and develop your manifest plan.

Now let's put your words into affirmations.

Positive Affirmations

An affirmation is a word, phrase or desire spoken affirmatively to bring your desire into manifestation.

An affirmation is a proclamation, a truth you claim, to affect your life. When you speak it with command, you can shift consciousness to positively change your physical world.

I first learned of affirmations as I began to study *Science of Mind* by Ernest Holmes. In 1984, Louise Hay, a Religious Science Practitioner published, *You Can Heal Your Life*, a guide to changing thoughts and beliefs. Hay's affirmations are designed to help the reader re-program their lives by changing their thoughts.

I love Louise Hay; she is truly a gift from God. I'm so proud to note this book is published by Balboa Press, a division of Hay House. Hay House is a publishing company she created to help others. If you don't own Louise Hay's book *You Can Heal Your Life*, buy it today! She remains one of my favorite authors, and her books are reread every year.

Change your thinking, and you change your life.

The Universe hears your words, your thoughts, picks up on your energies and what you focus on each day.

In Mark 11:24, KJV: "Therefore I tell you, whatever you ask in prayer, believe that you have received it, and it will be yours."

Invoke the "I am" power into your affirmations. Affirmations are shortened versions of prayer and will keep you from slipping into negative thoughts or feelings. They are one-liners that will help keep you motivated and focused.

To structure an affirmation on financial prosperity, say, "I am rich". If you can't internally accept that as truth, start with a statement you can mentally and emotionally accept, like, "I am getting richer every day".

At the end of every chapter, I have suggested affirmations. Feel free to use them or create your own.

When crafting your own affirmation, I recommend

beginning each affirmation by using I am. The more you repeat your affirmation, the more you will internally accept it, shaping your beliefs.

Fuse energy into each word. Energy is your power. And close your affirmation with Thank you Father-Mother-God or And So It is or end with a simple amen. However, when you close your affirmation or prayer, do it with real gratitude.

Add, "This or something better now manifests for me."

This is my go-to affirmation given to me by my first Religious Science Practitioner, Phyllis Proctor. It's as valid and inspired today as it was the day, she gave it to me. I have been using it for over 40 years ago. I am sure she is smiling at me from the spirit realm as I now share this wise affirmation with you.

"I am now led to a new life filled with more joy, more love, more prosperity, more health than I have ever imagined. And so, it is"

Affirmative Prayer

I first learned about scientific or affirmative prayer from Ernest Holmes and my Religious Science faith. Affirmative prayer is focused on an assured outcome. Ernest Holmes called this type of prayer scientific prayer or treatment work.

To understand affirmative prayer, I'd like to remind you of how Jesus prayed. When Jesus brought Lazarus back from the dead, He didn't ask God to hear His prayer,
He didn't beg. He simply knew God is always listening. Jesus spoke His word with confidence and conviction, "Lazarus, come forth!" KJV, John 11:43. And, Lazarus rose from the dead.

Begin your affirmative prayer by setting your intention or stating your desired outcome.

After stating your intention, you acknowledge God. I say it this way, "God is omnipresence, omni powerful. God is life.

God is Love. God is health. God is prosperity. God is One with all Life."

I then acknowledge myself as part of this Oneness by saying: "I am One with that Infinite Mind. I am this love. I am this Life. I am this Love. I am one, unified with God."

I restate my intention. "Today, I speak my word for health."

Give thanks with an attitude of gratitude. Say "Thank you, Father-Mother-God" with the knowingness that your prayer is already answered.

Last but not least, release your prayer by letting it go, knowing it will be done and add, "This or something better now manifests for me."

When I passed out assignments to my staff, I didn't check on them or micromanage their progress throughout the day. I gave them their assignments and walked away, assured they would follow through on their assignments.

The same is true when you release your prayer or request to the Universe. Release it and know you have done your part. Let the Spirit do its work.

I am a writer. I think best in words, and so I write my prayers in a journal.

I'd like to recommend for affirmation and for an affirmative prayer book, I recommend *Your Needs Met* by Jack and Cornelia Addington or *Heal your Life* by Louise Hay. There are a number of other wonderful books on prosperity and affirmation. Find one that works for you, or certainly write out your own.

As we move onto the next chapter, I have some tips and tools to help you keep your consciousness and energy high.

CHAPTER 5
Manifestation Tools

You do not have to use the manifest tools I include in this chapter. However, I have found that the manifestation tools listed can be practical, positive, uplifting reminders to help you stay optimistic and confident during manifestation.

When I have recommended them to others, my clients return and share their experienced manifestation faster as these tools keep them focused on their desires.

Talisman

Amulets or talismans have been used for centuries by wizards, master magicians and everyday folk like you and me. Talismans were blessed and infused with magic or intention.

The use of amulets dates back to 25,000 BC. Amber beads were discovered in Britain 10,000 years ago, the end of the last ice age. Jet beads, bracelets and necklaces have been discovered in Paleolithic gravesites in Switzerland and Belgium. Malachite amulets found in Sinai date to 4000 BC.

Amulets and Talisman were officially banned by the Catholic church in 355 A.D. However, in their place, the early church encouraged members to carry and use rosaries, prayer beads, a crucifix, or holy pendants bearing the image of a Saint or the Virgin Mary. Like their forerunners, these beautiful and precious objects are meant to bring the owner comfort, protection and strengthen their relationship with God.

We don't call them talismans anymore; we call them lucky charms. We carry a rabbit's foot, four-leaf clover, a lucky penny, and sometimes we place a horse shoe above the entrance of our homes for good luck.

I use talismans to fast-track my desires from the etherical plane into the manifest plane. They are visual reminders of that which I wish to manifest.

Your talisman does not have to be expensive, and it may be something you already possess.

Once when working with a client, he desired to manifest a new car. His mother's old station wagon was on its last legs. He wanted a Mercedes-Benz. It was his dream car. To help him keep his focus uppermost in his mind, I suggested he buy a Mercedes-Benz key chain. He was receptive to the idea and purchased a key chain. Every time he saw it or touched it, he was affirmed he would own his dream car. Within a year, he was.

Manifestation can happen instantly or take time as your mind and emotional energy must align with your desire.

When another client longed for a loving companion, I suggested she purchase a locket. No one knew its significance, and she quietly wore her locket close to her heart. She put a picture of her ideal man in the locket and toyed with her locket during business meetings, watching TV or any stray moment in time. Every time she touched it, she was mentally connecting to her desire.

At the moment, I am working on manifesting paying off my home. With this intention, I have an engraved key chain that says "Thank you Father-Mother-God" on one side and on the flip side, it reads "My home paid in full". Every time I touch it, I affirm my home is paid in full with an attitude of gratitude. Every time I leave the house or drive my car, I am gently reminded that my home is paid in full.

Your talisman can be anything that keeps your mind focused on your desire. Your talisman can be anything that reminds you of your desire. You don't need to advertise your dream to everyone because sometimes sharing your dream with the wrong person can open yourself up to ridicule. No one is going to notice the little charm on your keychain or a locket around your neck.

If you desire is to go to Jamacia or any other destination,

have fun with it. Visit the destination you desire, download pictures and arrange them in a photo book to help you visualize, listen to the country's music and dance, and dine at local Caribbean restaurants. No one will question your travel poster in your office or home. All of these things are to keep your dream at the top of your mind, and bring it close to reality. They are a fun item that keeps you focused on your desire.

Another fun way to help you focus on your dream is by creating a photo book to reference during the day or before bed each night.

A photo book is similar to a treasure map as you slide in pictures of that which you desire. As you focus on the photos, in prayer and thought, you are focusing on the answer. The Universe is watching, and like my little carrousel, when you pray, release and with gratitude, the Universe will respond.

A Photobook, A Magic Box

A photo book is a little photo album that will take a little time to collect the pictures you desire, but it's a lovely little memento of the here, and now that is soon to be.

In this instance, you start with the answer and allowing the Universe to bring what you desire into the manifest plane.

I have a photo book I look at in the morning and before bed with the photos of items I want to desire. You can purchase small plastic photo books at Walmart or the Dollar Store.

I had a lot of fun filling my photo book with the desire of my dreams and wishes. I have the picture of what I desire, and on the opposite page, I'll write an affirmation, such as "Thank you, Father-Mother-God, for my desire."

Please note, these are my words. You are more than welcome to use them or write your own affirmation. You can substitute God, Jesus, the Universe.

Years ago, I also found online a woman author seated in her home office. My affirmation reads, "Thank you Father-Mother-God for my I am able to work from home." Which happily, I am doing now.

You can put an image of a business, a home, a bride and groom, children, anything you desire into your photo book.

A photo book takes a little time to gather the right pictures but is worth it. An alternative is a "magic or treasure box".

I write down the things I want, fold them up and put them in my treasure box. My wishes and desires are my intentions.

With your desires written down, let the Universe deliver on your desire.

Two thousand years ago, the fulfillment of your desire would have been called a miracle. Today, we can say manifestation. Dreams do come true; you are the magic that makes it happen.

I use crystals in mediation, prayer, healing work and, of course, manifestation work.

Crystals

Dear Reader, I want to remind you that this book, the author or the publisher are not medical professionals. The intent of the author and this book is only to provide you with information of a general nature to help you in your quest for emotional and spiritual wellbeing and general information.

If you use any of the information in this book for yourself, which is your constitutional right, the author and the publisher assume no responsibility.

As I am writing this chapter, three articles came across my Facebook Newsfeed on the healing properties of crystals. I have found using crystals effective, and my primary care physician is aware of my use of them. He smiles when I tell him, but he respects my faith and belief.

The worldwide interest in crystals is growing, and this interest is reflected as prices for precious gemstones and crystals are rising. News outlets like *The Guardian* and others predict that prices for crystals, precious gems, and minerals will double or even triple in the next several years.

Modern science debunks the use of crystals for healing but yet uses crystals in communication devices from radios to computer chips, circuits, medical imaging devices, and satellites is a common practice. Science has been using crystals in lasers since the 1960s.

Crystals are used in every communication device known to man. Why then can't they be used in communicating with the Divine?

Throughout the centuries, shopkeepers and retailers routinely kept a citrine crystal in their cash resisters. You will still find a beautiful citrine in modern-day cash registers to draw in abundance.

Tapping into crystal energy dates back centuries to the ancient Sumerians, who included crystals in magic formulas. The Egyptians used lapis lazuli, carnelian, emerald and clear quartz in their jewelry, and they were favorites when creating amulets for health, love and protection.

Crystals are mentioned throughout the Bible, the Koran and many other religious texts. The Book of Exodus, in particular, states crystals were worn on the breastplate of Aaron, or the "High Priest's Breastplate". This breastplate contained twelve crystals, each representing the twelve tribes of Israel. It was worn by the High Priest when in holy communication with God.

The Mayans and Aztecs used crystals. The Zunis tribe fashioned fetishes and made jewelry of precious gems. The predominant colors and stones used by the Zuni are turquoise, red coral, black jet, and white mother of pearl. Symbolically, red represents Mother Earth and turquoise Father Sky.

Both Aborigines and Māori have traditions regarding stones and healing or spiritual practice. Some of them share with the rest of the world, while some knowledge is still kept private within their communities.

Crystals were used across centuries, in different

times, continents, cultures and civilizations who had no communication with one another and yet independently used the same type of crystals for specialized healings.

Both the ancient Chinese and the Aztec and Mayans tapped into the mystical healing powers of jade and other crystals. These two civilizations were an ocean away from the other, and there is no known contact between them, yet both cultures used many of the same types of crystals for the same purposes. Was it coincidence, or did the healing powers of the crystals make themselves known to the master healers of these [powerful empires?

Albert Einstein said, "Everything is energy and that's all there is to it. This is not philosophy. This is physics."

Energy is found in every living thing. Even our planet has its own electromagnetic field. Crystals have energy. Plants have energy. In fact, even our planet vibrates with energy.

Humans have our own unique frequency or vibrational energy, which can be influenced by the weather, tides, moon phases, and emotions.

Crystal energy is fixed and stable. Rocks also have a low-frequency energy. When the sun shines on them, they absorb the sun's energy, become warm, and create and emulate heat.

Ancient healers used crystals for healing, manifesting, communicating with the Divine, and drawing in prosperity and protection.

You don't need scientific data to validate the energy and frequency of crystals. You can do that yourself by merely holding one.

I am a crystal intuitive, which it's easy for me to pick up the energy and vibration of crystals. Many people like myself can pick up the vibration of a crystal by touch. Some people don't immediately experience the vibrational of crystals, and that's okay. To those people, I would suggest practice makes perfect. I don't understand how an automobile engine works, but if I put my key into the ignition switch, the car will roar to life and take me to my destination.

Besides their natural beauty, crystals can store and amplify energy.

You can use crystals in the manifestation process to amplify your intensity, help you make the divine connection between the etherical plane and the manifest plane and harass and direct your energy.

I use crystals daily in the process of clearing my chakras and during meditation. I use crystals to connect and amplify the healing process. I use crystals to manifest my desire.

There are thousands and thousands of crystals available to you. As my husband often tells me, use the right tool for the right job.

As a general rule, citrine is primarily used for prosperity and abundance. Malachite or Aventurine is used for healing, and Rose Quartz is a favorite of the energy of love.

I recommend crystals at the end of every chapter. Use them for your own clarity, divine connection, as a calming stone or when manifesting what you desire.

If you are looking for a quality source of crystals, I highly recommend Debbie Hardy. She is a trusted source of high-quality but very affordable crystals and offers a wide variety of crystals to choose. Debbie is an author, Certified Crystal Healer, Advanced Crystal Master and Reiki Master. You can contact Debbie through her website at www.hardycrystalblessing.com

In this chapter we have explored the use of talismans, crystals and imagery to aid in your manifestation. I use them because I have found them effective in keeping my conscious mind focused and on point as I manifest my dreams. I always turn to God and prayer. The choice of using talismans, prayer or crystals is up to you.

At the end of each chapter, I will suggest an affirmation, perhaps a crystal or two and or a fun talisman to help you with your dreams. If you see value in helping you stay focused, by all means, use them if you like.

Do all you can to uplift your sense of worthiness and self-confidence, for I know as truth, you are a child of God, and you deserve to have a wonderful life filled with every good thing.

The publisher and myself and anyone associated with this book do not advise you to use crystals, talismans or imagery or visualizations as a substitute for medical advice. If you need a doctor, see a doctor. I do. I use my talisman and crystals to aid in my healing and prosperity work to accelerate the process.

Whether you use a rosary, a set of prayer beads, a key chain, or any other talisman for comfort or luck, it is entirely up to you, but I personally find them a fun item to keep me focused on manifesting my dreams and my goals.

I highly recommend Debbie Hardy. She is a trusted source of high-quality but very affordable crystals and offers a wide variety of crystals to choose. Debbie is an author, Certified Crystal Healer, Advanced Crystal Master and Reiki Master. You can contact Debbie through her website at www.hardycrystalblessing.com

CHAPTER 6 HEALTH

Five years ago, the doctors found a dark lump in my breast and validated the image in an x-ray. I was asked to return a month later to ascertain its growth.

When I reached my home, I immediately turned to prayer. I called on Archangel Raphael and his healing Angels. As I prayed, I held green aventurine crystals in the palms of my hands and placed a third crystal where the lump was in my breast. Every day, I prayed. I used the power of visualization. Through my guided imagery, I saw the lump dissolve and leave my body. I aligned my energy to perfect health.

I returned to the clinic at my appointed time. My new sonogram caused quite a stir among the technicians who rushed in two doctors to authenticate their findings. The mass was no longer there. The previous month's x-rays hung on a viewing glass. The black mass was clearly visible. The doctors and technicians were completely baffled. I was not. I knew God had answered my prayer, and I was the recipient of Divine intervention.

This wasn't the first time I had this type of healing. In 2007, my doctor found a lump on my thyroid. A lump that disappeared a month later. To my thinking, this was not a miracle. This was the expected outcome of a healing manifestation.

Faith healings are often referred to as miracles and, for the most part, mystify medical professionals.

Jesus performed over 40 healings in the New Testament.

The early Christian church-sanctioned faith healing. They practiced faith healing through prayer and included techniques such as anointing the head or body with oil or the laying on of hands.

Today people still make pilgrimages to sacred sites worldwide where they are healed through the power of prayer and their beliefs.

Medical miracles are by no means restricted to the Christian faith. They are found in every religion, faith and practice worldwide.

Faith healings date back centuries. Ancient healers used mystical arts, herbal medicines and tapped into the celestial power of sacred geometry and crystals.

We are turning to back to those ancient healing methods, and old wives' tales are being revisited.

There are a number of books with the title Food as Medicine.

One of my favorite streaming networks is *Gaia*. *Gaia* offers numerous programs on healing to include tapping, information on acupressure, sound, meditation, food, yoga, use of essential oils, dietary supplements and vitamins, vibration therapy and an endless array of healing modalities.

The World Health Organization stated in 2008 that an estimated range from 70% to 80% of the world population looks to alternative and holistic medicines. Modern science is starting to recognize and appreciate these once forgotten healing methods.

This chapter is about helping you understand the mind-body-spirit connection but is in no way a substitute for medical treatment, advice or assistance.

As I mentioned previously, I have the good fortune to see a wonderful doctor who listens to me and looks at me during every visit. I take his advice and the prescriptions he recommends. However, I also look to holistic practices to complement his diagnosis and treatment.

The holistic and natural remedies include but are not limited to Acupuncture, Chinese and Oriental medicine, yoga, Tai Chi and dietary supplements.

Yoga is a 6000-year-old, time tested practice that

combines stretching, breathing and helps with muscle relaxation. I use yoga to elevate pain from my back and shoulders and relieve sciatica, which no longer troubles me. Yoga builds upper and lower body strength, straightens the core and brings the body and the spine back into alignment.

Countless athletics have used visualization and guided imagery to help them achieve successful outcomes and with sports injuries.

I am not a doctor or medical professional, but as a Christian and I personally have experienced the power of prayer.

Talk to your doctor before beginning any alternative holistic practice to make sure it complements what the doctor is recommending and will not alter the prescriptions you are given.

Pray as your faith prescribes and use affirmations to use to help you in your journey.

In Louise Hay's beautiful book, *You Can Heal Your Life,* her message is: "If we are willing to do the mental work, almost anything can be healed." Louise Hay goes into depth and shares her firsthand experience, including how she cured herself after being diagnosed with cancer. Ernest Holmes wrote You *Can Heal Your Life* and *The Science of Mind.* I recommend all three books.

Both Ernest Holmes and Louise Hay discuss mental causes of illness and express that as you change your thinking, you can change your life.

This book aims to help you fulfill your dreams of a happy, healthy, joy-filled and prosperous life through the power of the Law of Attraction.

This book in no way should be viewed as a substitute for medical advice. Always consult a licensed medical practitioner. The author nor the publisher can be held responsible for any loss, claim or damage arising from the use or misuse of the suggestions made or any material to any third-party websites directly or indirectly. The intent of the author is only to offer information of a general nature to help you in your quest for emotional and spiritual wellbeing.

Below, you will find a visualization affirmation to help you maintain and achieve good health.

As you read through the visualization, feel free to change or use your own.

Visualization

Sit with your feet squarely on the ground. Take deep yoga breaths to calm your body and align your body with the healing energy of the Universe. (Yoga breathes slow breaths, taking in air to the count of eight, holding the breath for three seconds, and then releasing the breath to the count of eight.)

As you close your eyes, you are aware of the Divine spark of your own Divinity within you. You allow this glimmer of light to grow from a tiny sparkle deep within you to a dazzling radiance that floods your body with beautiful light. You are the light in the darkness. Your beauty and pure goodness are breathtaking, and you realize now more than ever before that you are one with the Universe and one with God.

You are conscious of slivery roots growing from your feet down into the earth. As they travel down, you notice the rich, brown color of the earth and become aware of the bright multi-colors of gemstones buried in the dirt. Bright flashes of diamonds and shimmering strands of gold, silver and rich red copper shine in the earth and granite. Your shimmering roots travel down until they reach a vast cavern of glittering crystals of light that fully illuminate the grotto with bright light. You realize you are at the earth's core and standing below the Tree of Life. You allow your roots to anchor to a large stone in the center of the room and then rise to center with your physical body.

Safe, secure in your visualization, you slowly open your mind's eye and realize with delight at you are standing before the great Temple of Raphael, the Healing Temple of Atlantis.

Long-marbled stairs rise to the huge alabaster columns that glisten white in the sunlight. This massive Greco-Roman structure dominates the landscape.

You slowly climb and find several beautiful young ladies waiting at the top. They hurry down to meet you and welcome you into the sacred space.

The attendants usher you across polished marbled floors are polished to a room off the main entrance. The inside of the temple is open, and at the far end, you can see fluffy white clouds as they glide across a soft turquoise sky.

The young girls open the door and leave you. Two beautiful beings approach you, and you know them as Angels. They guide you to a changing room. A moment later, you return to the healing chamber. You are now dressed in a comfortable gown.

You're first invited to step into a small tropical waterfall. As you enter a cascade of clear, sparkling waterfalls upon you, gently washing away the stress and any tension you feel. When you feel clean and fully relaxed, free of all worry and worldly burdens, you step out of the shower and are asked to lie atop a very comfortable raised massage table.

You settle atop the mattress, where you are exceedingly comfortable and lie in perfect peace.

The Healing Angels approach you and, in your visualization, you close your eyes. They slowly begin to scan your body, pausing in areas where you need healing.

As they move about, you feel your body become stronger and healthier.

Anything that is not meant to be in your body is removed painlessly, easily and as it leaves your body. It turns in wisps of smoke to vanish in the healing energy of the room. You can stay on the lounge relaxing for several minutes, and when you are ready, the healers invited to you step into a green emerald crystal bath.

The water is soothing and healing, and you can remain here for as long as you like.

When you are ready, you are escorted to a beautiful healing garden. It is filled with an extraordinary array of flowers. The sun is dancing off each petal, and it is warm to your skin. You follow a soft green path to a small calm pool.

In the shade of a beautiful cheery tree, a small wooden bench awaits you.

You can sit, rest, and relax for as long as you wish in this beautiful garden.

When you are ready to leave, you thank God, the Universe, for this healing experience and the peace that fills you.

This or something greater now manifests in my life, and so it is.

When you are ready, slowly open your eyes and your heart.

You send love and healing energy to the world. And begin your day or fall into a restful sleep in your bed.

Affirmations

1. I am whole, healthy, perfect and complete.
2. I embrace health. I live a healthy lifestyle.
3. I release all negative thoughts. I am fully open to the healing energy of God.
4. Perfect health is my birthright.
5. I give thanks to the Universe for my radiant health. God's healing energy flows through my body in loving, good health.
6. I eat only healthy foods, think only positive thoughts and lovingly treat my body with care.
7. I am healthy, strong, whole and complete. I am open and receptive to all the healing energies in the Universe.
8. I love and honor myself by maintaining good health every day in every way.
9. I release any thoughts that tell me I am unworthy of good health. I embrace good health, love and enjoy my healthy lifestyle.
10. Thank you, Father-Mother-God, for my good health.

Crystals

For thousands of years, humanity has turned to crystals to help heal, health and general wellbeing.

There are countless crystals for specific medical diagnoses.

For example, when I tap or meditate and visualize, I will hold a girasol in each palm for diabetes. Girasol is used when working with diabetes and the immune system. When I work in alleviating symptoms of rheumatoid arthritis, I will work with a carnelian.

If you have a specific condition, a crystal healer or practitioner can help you select the ideal crystals to assist you in your treatment and or recovery.

The following crystals are favorites to aid in general health and wellbeing.

Clear Quartz

Clear quartz is referred to as the master healer and carries strong vibrational energy. Clear quartz stimulates immune systems and helps to align the chakras.

Clear quartz is a crystal of connection and will help in all communication types, including the Divine. Clear Quartz is often used both in channeling and when meditating.

As its names implies, this master healer can be used for just about any condition and bring the body into balance.

Green Aventurine

One of my go-to favorites for healing is green aventurine. While this crystal is used in attracting financial abundance and prosperity, green aventurine also promotes healing, wellbeing and emotional calm.

Many select green aventurines when working with the Heart Chakra. It is a wonderful crystal for general wellbeing and emotional calm.

Malachite

Another favorite of mine is Malachite. Malachite is associated with the heart chakra and opens the heart to love.

Malachite absorbs negative energies and pollutants, guards against electromagnetic pollution, releases negative experiences, and stimulates the immune system.

If you are looking for a particular crystal to use during meditation or visualization, I suggest you look for a Crystal Healer or Crystal Intuitive in your area. There are also several books available on crystal Healing. *The Crystal Bible* by Judy Hall is a favorite in the crystal community.

The Crystal Bible is a comprehensive and beautifully illustrated guide to crystals with detailed descriptions and the properties and meanings of each crystal.

The information in this book should not be treated as a substitute for medical advice. Always consult a licensed medical practitioner. The author nor the publisher can be held responsible for any loss, claim or damage arising out of the use or misuse of the suggestions made or any material to any third-party websites.

CHAPTER 8
MANIFESTING LOVE

If you fully and completely love yourself, skip this section. If you don't love yourself or know even where to begin, these next few pages are for you. You see, before we start attracting a soulmate, your perfect twin flame, you must love yourself.

Love is an inside job.

You will not attract a wonderful man or woman into your life without first loving the wonderful person you see in the mirror.

As you move through this section, may I suggest you keep a notebook to record your thoughts and feelings?

If you feel desperately lonely, if your energy screams for another to make you whole, please be aware that another person will not fill that empty place in your heart or make you complete.

I get it. I've been there, done that, and understand that during the initial blush of romantic love, you do feel complete by your new paramour. However, as the relationship ages, the instability and feelings of unworthiness once again bubble as the demons of jealousy, fear, and mistrust will rise to the surface. These emotions will play their part in the destruction of your relationship. You are not alone as you enter this phase, for the they will likewise be unable to hold their façade, and the illusion of what could be, should be will vanish like wisps of smoke before your eyes.

If you have insecurities, you will attract a partner who has insecurities. If you are insecure, you will attract someone equally jealous or give you something to be jealous about. Two broken, scared, insecure people will not make each other or the relationship whole.

Two whole, self-confident people will create a solid relationship build in trust, kindness and love.

My childhood memories are filled with mental and sometimes physical abuse. Without proper therapy, I grew into womanhood feeling unlovable, unworthy of love and desperately looking for someone to save me from myself. My personal lessons were filled with tears, physical bruises and mental scars marked with a lot of pain. I had always dreamed of that knight in shining armor. However, because of my low self-esteem, I opened my heart to the first guy who crossed my path on a donkey. My self-image was perfectly reflected in the men I choose and by my feelings of unworthiness.

A fairy godmother will not appear to create a royal match for you unless and until you recognize your worth. You, my dear friend, are of royal blood.

How show love to yourself? Where do you begin? Be kind and realize, for many of us, no one every explained how or even why we should love ourselves.

The first step on this path is to stop judging and criticizing yourself. While you are at it, stop judging others. Live in a judgment free zone. This includes yourself, your past mistakes and any bad choices you made. Remember, at each turn in the road, you made the very best choices you could base on the information you had at the time.

You are a little older now and a lot wiser. In your newfound wisdom, you would now make different choices. So, release the past. It's over. Release any regrets you may have. Let them go. The past will no longer play a role in your future if you let it go. Forgive yourself, forgive all others and release those memories.

If you don't release and let go of these memories, these experiences will return to you because you keep holding onto them.

As I have stated many times, the Universe is listening to your thoughts and energy. If you dwell on past these negative memories, you will be given another opportunity to repeat them. Instead, focus on your present peace as you learn to love yourself.

Next, let's set boundaries. Realize it's a privilege for anyone to be invited into your personal space and your life. This privilege must be earned.

You are looking for a partner who will compliment your life, not take it over and consume you with his interests.

At the end of one of my unhappy relationships, my very wise counselor, after listening to me ramble on and on about my ex and how my life was nothing without him, asked, "What do you like to do?"

I was thunderstruck!

To my complete embarrassment, I could not remember a hobby or interest that I personally enjoyed. It took me three days, three days to remember I liked to read books. It took me another week to remember I had always wanted to be a writer, own a horse and enjoy nature without the abrasive sound of motorized vehicles.

In the following years, I brought two horses. I renewed my interest in outdoor adventures, and I began not only to read but to write. To my complete joy, I found and re-discovered myself.

What brings you joy? What did you want to do as a child? Do a self-inventory and see yourself worthy of persuading your dreams.

Once a client announced to be his dream was to be an Insurance Broker. "Really," I asked, "when you were six years old, you wanted to be an insurance broker?"

It took a few more minutes before he admitted, "I always wanted to be in a position where I could help people."

As he focused his attention on becoming a therapist, the light returned to his eyes and, today, he has a beautiful practice where he helps people every day. There is nothing wrong with being an insurance broker but discover what brings fire to your soul a job, career or profession that makes you count the hours till sunrise each day. There is an old saying, do what you love, and you will never work a day in your life.

Do things that you enjoy and be a little selfish. Do what brings you joy.

Doing things that you love is an important part of feeling worthy. Don't allow yourself to become lost in someone else's life. Doing things, you love will light the path in celebrating you.

I'd like you to create a list of what you love about yourself. Your list should include the wonderful qualities and characteristics you admire and appreciate about yourself.

When I began my list, my self-esteem was so low, I could only think of one thing I liked about myself. Very reluctantly, almost grudgingly, I thought I had pretty blue eyes. It took me another month before I could begin to add to my list.

With pride, I discovered I was a loyal friend. I had an abundance of kindness. As I wrote my list, a picture began to form of someone worthy of love. It was me!

Write your list. Appreciate the qualities and traits that make you great.

Develop a deep appreciation of who you are by acknowledging your strengths, acknowledging your courage, your connection to life, what you have endured and survived to reach your present place in this world. This is no small thing. You will discover you are wise, kind, talented, a great cook, a great listener and a terrific friend. In fact, this person who stares at you in the mirror is quite amazing.

You will come to understand that the person you are writing about is one of value and worth. Stop looking at yourself through the eyes of others. You were never the ugly duckling; you were always a magnificent and beautiful swan!

Take back the power you gave to other people and learn to give that love and attention to yourself. This is not selfish, it's self-survival. This gift you give yourself lays the foundation for a beautiful life that you will share with a beautiful companion.

Make love an action verb in your life.

Take time to love and enjoy your body, and your body, in turn, will respond.

Treat yourself to good foods. Internalize this affirmation, "I love myself; therefore, I nurture my body with healthy foods." Your body will return the favor with health.

Do loving little things for yourself. For example, put candles around your bath, a beautiful fragrance in your bath water and find music to relax you. Do this because you are worth it. This small loving gesture speaks volumes to your soul.

If a relaxing bath is not for you, find something that is. Treat yourself with love.

Spend time in nature. As you walk, notice the flowers, the birds singing or the stars in the heavens shining down on you.

Mediate and if you don't know how to meditate, learn how.

Start to love yourself with these little activities as you learn that you are worth such pleasures and such good until you realize you are participating in this beautiful life that is yours.

You don't have to be perfect at loving yourself in the beginning. You were not born with low self-esteem, and those feelings didn't happen overnight, so be aware this is a journey, not a sprint. It may take time to turn these feelings around.

There are a lot of self-help books available to you that tell you why to love yourself. What I am suggesting is an action plan.

You will learn how to love yourself by doing loving things.

By doing that which you enjoy and find pleasure in, you will see that you are indeed worthy of a magnificent love story where you are a star. The Universe is watching and supporting this new vision of yourself, and the result will be to bring into the manifest plane that you desire.

As you built this strong foundation, you simultaneously send out the vibration of a confident, self-assured man or woman. The Universe will return a companion who is worthy of you. Like attracts like.

It's now time to focus, align and manifest a wonderful partner in your life. You are going to mastermind an action plan based on the love and appreciation you give yourself.

Attracting Your Perfect Partner

In your desire to find a loving companion, I recommend you think about exactly what characteristics you desire in a partner. Be as specific and detailed as possible and start practicing these attributes today.

Write down the attributes you want in a partner. I am going to assume; you want someone kind. This person should be kind to you, kind to his parents, kind to animals and kind to everyone who comes into his or her life. As you begin a courtship with this person, watch how he treats the waitress, his secretary, his or her mother or the homeless person he passes by.

As your relationship grows, be diligent and don't overlook the red flags he or she throws in your path.

Once, I went on a date with an attorney, who treated me as if I were spun gold. At lunch one day, he was horrible to the waitress who was working by herself in a crowded restaurant. He berated her in front of anyone because she had put his salad dressing on the salad instead of serving it on the side. I felt horrible for his atrocious behavior and mistreatment of the waitress. I was embarrassed by him. It took me a half-second to fast forward his behavior to a time in the future when my son didn't fold his socks properly and would bear the attorney's harsh reprimand. He was not for me and not for my son!

I apologized to the waitress, left her a big tip and said goodbye to this rich, handsome attorney and his black heart. I refused to take his calls. Pay attention because how he treats others for this is how he will one day treat you.

Your future companion must treat you with respect, understanding and integrity.

High on my personal list is a sense of humor. It's my experience humor and laughter are keystones in making a pleasurable life. After 21 years of a happy marriage, my husband still makes me laugh. There have been challenges in our relationship, but kindness to one another, respect and laughter got us through the rough waters.

Your person should be a compassionate soul and be open to communication and compromise.

As you work on your list, write down your deal points and breakpoints.

When I was finally ready to find a worthy companion for myself, I wrote down my own list of deal points and breakpoints. For me, a deal-breaker was someone who used illegal drugs and or was a smoker. With a young child at home, I did not want a smoker.

Deal point was I felt it was okay for my partner to enjoy a beer after work with his friends. A deal breaker was someone who practically lived at the bar.

For me, a deal breaker is someone who cheated in a past relationship or hit or abused a child or a woman. These were red flags for me.

I am very involved in the New Age philosophy. In my writing, personal beliefs and interests revolve around a New Age lifestyle. While I was open to anyone's personal faith, if he felt my New Age lifestyle were akin to devil worship, I knew it would be a deal-breaker. I find my God in prayer and meditation. My husband finds God in nature and respects my beliefs and choices. Deal point.

If your political or religious views are diametrically opposite, look for common ground. Please think twice before you compromise who you are for someone else. I promise you, the little things you are willing to overlook in the initial phase of your relationship will become monsters at the end of it.

Write down what you enjoy and what are must-haves in your life. I choose to live and be surrounded by animals so, must love dogs is high on my list.

I love the outdoors. I am an environmentalist, and happily so is my husband.

My ideal night out for me is sitting in front of an open

fire in the woods. A sophisticated evening at the museum or theater is not for me. If you enjoy watching a Broadway musical, write down your preferences and know you will be living your choices, so make sure the two of you are aligned with a lifestyle you enjoy.

What are your music preferences? Country western, jazz or don't care. Put that on your list.

Think on and focus on every attribute and or trait you can think of or imagine.

Last but not least, when you see the guy that surprises his wife in a television commercial with jewelry, don't envision that because that guy is not in your life, but rather, identify with the handsome man and say to yourself, my husband will treat me with way because I am worth it.

When you see a loving couple dining out, don't think, I will never have such a beautiful relationship; think, that's my life, or that's my life now.

Do not try to change another person. Listen carefully to what they say and accept the person for who they are.

A friend cried when her husband refused to have a baby with her. Throughout their courtship, he told her over and over again, he did not want children. She should have listened. She held the erroneous opinion that once they were married, she could change his mind. She could not change his mind, and they wound up getting a divorce. Listen to what your potential husband or wife says to you. If you see red flags, find the courage within yourself to walk away. Be assured, there is someone better for you out there, and trust the Universe to make it so.

Lastly, have fun with a bit of planning. What does Sunday morning to look like at your house? Do you both attend church or wear pajamas while you read the Sunday paper.

What are your hobbies? Do not give up being you, which includes your hobbies and interests.

If you like sports, put that on your list. If you hate sports and he loves sports, decide if you can comprise by joining him by watching a game or use that time to enjoy your personal pursuits.

Allow for compromise or acceptance. Decide if your partner's choices are a deal point for you or a breakpoint.

Once you have your ideal mate with all his attributes and characteristics, it's time to manifest him in your life.

Remember, the Universe is always watching and listening.

The following affirmations and visualizations included are suggestions. Use them or create your own.

Visualizations

Sit with your feet squarely on the ground. Take deep yoga breaths to calm your body and align your body with the energy of love.

As you close your eyes, you breathe in love, peace and happiness. With each exhale, breathe out any regrets, false beliefs of being unlovable, letting go of the past, releasing any worries about the future. Continue to breathe in and out until only serenity and peace remain. In this stilled moment, now and forever, you are now open to love. Deep within you, you are aware of a warm glow of love. You allow it to rise and spread throughout your body, filling every cell with your loving energy.

In your mind's eye, as you begin your visualization, you open your eyes and realize you are standing in before a movie theater. You see your name in the marquis and are excited to watch the wonderful coming attractions of your life.

You walk up to the window, and the ticket person smiles at you and hands you a ticket.

As you enter the theater, the lobby is alive with excitement, and you see people milling around. They are all here to celebrate the story of you.

As you walk past the concession stand, you catch the heady aroma of movie popcorn and hear the sound of ice falling into a plastic cup. There is distinct anticipation in the air because the lights flicker, signaling the movie is about to start.

As you walk past the ticket taker, he points to the shows playing. Again, you see your name in the theater lights.

You walk into the theater and take the best seat in the house. It's comfortable, and as you get settled in, the lights dim, the theater goes black, and the screen lights up.

You watch the story begin to unfold. You see yourself in various stages of your life, and then the main feature begins with the person who is your life partner.

The story opens with you and your true love walking through a park. You are months into your relationship now. As you walk through the park, you are distinctly aware of the bird singing high above in the tress and the soft fragrance of flowers.

In the distance, you hear the laughter of children and see a group of people playing ball. You pass an old couple sitting on a park bench, and your partner looks at you and smiles. For one day, far into the future, you will be looking into one another's eyes still in love, and with memories of the magical life you will share.

The scene changes to you and your lover at a fine restaurant. The waiter is coming toward you with a cake. Atop the cake, sparkling candles brighten the room. Everyone in the restaurant is smiling and clapping. Your partner has arranged this lovely birthday surprise for you, and after you blow out the candles, he presents you with a beautiful necklace that says I love you.

The scene changes again, it's fourth of July, and you watch the Fireworks in the comfort of his arms. As you watch the light show, you are filled with euphoria and joy.

The scene changes to winter, and you see your street. It's a quiet evening, and the snow at your feet is so soft, you do not even hear the crunch of your snowshoes.   Snowflakes continue to fall around you, and your hold your partner's hand. You feel peaceful and content.

A short time later, you and your partner sit front of a fireplace, feeling the warmth of the flames and the happiness of your home.

You continue to move through your life and see yourself and your family on vacations, running along the beach, lying together in a hammock, celebrating family dinners with friends and being carried across the door of your beautiful new home.

If you choose, you can see a baby in your life, watch with your husband as the baby takes their first steps. You see yourself cheering your child at soccer or baseball game. You can even go forward in your life to see yourself and your partner attending your adult child's wedding, exchanging the same vows you and your beloved spoke to one another.

You allow these scenes to unfold. You and your partner are experiencing the most beautiful life now.

The Universe brought you together in the most perfect way, and your happiness bubbles inside you.

As the movie comes to an end, you hold close to these visions, savoring each beautiful moment for the here and now that is soon to be.

You stay in this beautiful experience a moment longer before you slowly open your eyes, feeling loved, knowing love, and knowing this is your truth to love and be loved.

This beautiful love is now yours to experience. This or something better now manifests in your life. You celebrate this loving experience now.

As you see a man holding the door open for a female companion throughout the day, you identify with this scene for your partner always holds the door open for you. If you see a father playing or walking with kids, you know this joy is also yours to experience.

Before you sleep at night, you look up at the stars and know he or she is looking up to the same stars and again affirm, you are worthy of such love and that there is no delay with Divine plan for you.

If you have a moment throughout the day, you can return to this visualization with an attitude of gratitude because you are loved.

Affirmations

If preferred, you can say your affirmation at your scheduled times or every hour on the hour.

Below are affirmations that you can use, adapt, change or write your own.

1. I now activate the Law of Attraction, knowing I am worthy of a loving, perfect companion for me. I am open to giving and receiving love.
2. I trust the Universe to bring into my experience a loving and kind companion into my life today.
3. I am worthy of a beautiful, loving companion and a beautiful life.
4. I am open to experience a beautiful, loving relationship where I am loved, appreciated, treasured.
5. I now tighten the magical connection between me and my true love. I am in the right place at the right time to meet him. There is no delay in the Divine Plan for me.
6. I now connect to my perfect companion. My loving relationship is more than I can ever imagine.
7. I release the past and let love flow into my life. I am open to a new experience of more love, joy, kindness, and happiness than I have ever dreamed of. And so, it is.
8. I radiate with love. The more I love, the more loving thoughts, the closer my perfect companion is drawn to me.
9. I trust myself to make good choices in love and attract my forever partner, who is my best friend.
10. I release any past relationships, forgive myself and anyone involved, and let go of any former relationships that no longer serve me. In doing so, I have created a beautiful space for my perfect

soulmate.

11. I feel a deep union with my loved one. I trust the Universe to bring us together in a beautiful way. I am open to love.

Recommended Crystals

Rose Quartz

The universal favorite crystal of love is the Rose Quartz. This beautiful pink crystal holds within it the divine feminine energy that embraces all expressions of love.   From self-love to attracting a loving companion, the Rose Quartz will help open the heart to forgiveness of others and the self.

Rose Quartz is often the preferred crystal when working with the heart charka as it assists in elevating a loving vibration within you. As you radiate this loving energy, you align with love and with a loving companion.

Rhodochrosite

This is a rose-colored crystal that encourages emotional healing and bring love into your experience. For centuries, this beautiful crystal has been used in jewelry.

Rhodochrosite crystals also help to clear away and release any residual energy from past relationships and help open the heart to a love.

Moonstone

Moonstone is a great crystal for balancing and carries with it the beautiful energy of the moon. It's a crystal of new beginnings and aids in calming emotional energy. The moonstone helps us open up to love, energy and an abundance in all good things.

.   Men find the moonstone helpful in connecting with the emotional energy of love.

Talisman

Your talisman can be any small trinket or item that is a touchstone to keep your mind and emotions focused on manifesting a loving partner.

My preferred talisman for romance is a heart-shaped locket. If you use a locket, put a small picture of your ideal match on the inside or perhaps a couple in a wedding photo. Remember do not to outline with a specific someone.

As you move through your day or play with your locket during a business meeting or at a red light while you are driving, you are boosting your energy and bringing it into alignment with desire. No one is the wiser.

A ring, bracelet, or piece of jewelry work as well so keep your vision on the prize that awaits you and allow the power of love to fill you.

CHAPTER 9
Money, Wealth, Finances

Money, in and of itself, is neither good nor evil. Money is simply the commodity we currently use to acquire goods and services. Centuries ago, we were exchanging beads and seashells for goods and services.

After a time, we began bartering with one another. Bartering is exchanging the goods we created, such as bowls, knives, swords and bartering them for things we desired or needed.

The 20-dollar bill, in and of itself, is actually just paper. It represents a country's currency and the symbol of the gold and silver the world governments hold in their vaults. In the United States, our vault is commonly referred to as Fort Knox.

Much of our time on earth is spent acquiring money and then spending it.

Most people acquire money by working. They go to work at a company, and they receive a paycheck in exchange for their efforts. Some people create their own businesses, while others create wealth by investing in stocks or lands.

You accumulate wealth based on your alignment and personal association with your energy of abundance.

I have shared with you one of my favorite stories on wealth in a previous chapter. I am going to repeat it now because it so illustrates your truth about money.

You recall the story of the old lady whose husband left her for a younger woman, her ungrateful kids ran off, and her house was literally falling down around her. I was a

little taken back when the priest asked her, what had she asked God for? She had replied, why a roof over my head and a crust of bread. The universe listened to her energy, words, and thoughts and returned to her that she had focused upon.

You are the primary character in this story. The message in this story is, what have you asked of God? The treasure vaults of heaven were always open to you, if only you ask.

The poor lady in our story did not ask God for love, wealth and happiness. The Universe drew on her feelings of unworthiness and returned to her the corresponding effect.

"For as he thinketh in his heart, so is he", or she, as I paraphrase from Proverbs 23:7. KJV.

The Universe is impartial but will respond to what we focus on and perfectly return to your thoughts and feelings. If you focus on fear, lack of, and the negative, the Universe will not only respond in kind, sometimes give you more, for whatever you send out comes back multiplied.

Be mindful of the Law of Circulation. The Law of Circulation demands continuous flow. If you block the flow of money, you effectively halt the flow of financial abundance and block all good in your life. This happens when you feel unworthy or undeserving.

Blocking the flow is an insidious phenomenon inside you, one that you may or may not even be aware of. For instance, if you pass a homeless person on the street and you think, I don't have any extra money to give him; the Universe translates your thoughts and energy to mean you don't have money to spare. Watch your thinking. Watch your words. Watch your energy.

If you feel uncomfortable about accepting a gift or even a compliment, you block the flow.

Money needs to be in a constant state of flow. It's okay to add to your savings or hold onto it for a prosperous future; just don't hold onto it out of the fear that if you spend it, it won't return.

To break any fear or money blockage in your life, give. Give, give, give! Giving stimulates the Law of Circulation and galvanizes the Universe to create a fresh financial flow into your life.

You can't fill your glass with new wine if you don't throw away the old.

The next time you go into a restaurant or write a check, take a moment to experience the energy that flows out from you during this transaction. If you feel any self-limiting thoughts or concerns about money and release them until there is nothing left but gratitude for the meal you enjoyed.

Practice this activity until you feel delighted with the experience and the deep-seated knowingness that the money which you paid for your meal is now back in circulation and will return to you.

As you pay for a meal, see that money flowing from you to the server, the restaurant owner, and the farmer who buys and plants the seed. Feel the happiness of each exchange and the joy in each interaction by every person in the monetary chain. Watch your money move to the bankers and businesses and all the people who enjoy the happy benefit you set into motion. Feel the happiness of the employees who can make their house payment or buy toys for their children and food for their tables. The money, freely and lovingly given, will return to you, multiplied.

Learn to give and accept money with gratitude. Let go of any negative thoughts you have about money. Replace those thoughts with an attitude of gratitude by happily and joyfully accepting the funds, funds you are worthy to accept and experience.

Practice the act of gracious receiving. Be open to receiving money and learn how to say thank you as you receive it. To say anything other than thank you is to dishonor the giver. Thank the giver, thank God, and bless the funds.

Live in the Laws of Attraction and Circulation, and money, love, and abundance will flow continuously in your life.

Spend money with joy and pleasure and a knowingness it will return. This does not in any way mean you are to frivolously charge your credit cards, but rather when you do spend it, do so without restriction or lack.

So, when did we begin to have an issue with money? For many of us, this fear of money began when we were children.

I was terrified when I heard at Sunday School that money was evil, and if I loved money, I wouldn't go to heaven. Yikes, I wanted to go to heaven! I was also frightened by monsters under my bed and noises outside my window.

As I grew, I realized the monsters weren't real, there was no such thing as the boogeyman, and if I hear scraping against the house, I know now it's time to trim the trees.

Yet, the concept that money was in and of itself as being evil lingered in the dark recesses of my subconscious mind. It was compounded by the often-heard declarations from my parents that I was unworthy. Over time, the fear of money and the belief that I was unworthy of money assimilated my psyche.

This feeling, this fear, this negative energy grew roots and blocked my path to financial abundance for many years.

Gradually and over time, I realized I was a beloved child of God, worthy of every good thing. It took countless books, tapes, and CDs, as well as a lot of internal dialogue and hard work, to eradicate my thoughts and feelings of unworthiness.

Learn to give and receive money with joy and gratitude. Practice the act of gracious receiving. Be open to receiving money and learn how to say thank you as you receive. To say anything other than thank you is to dishonor the giver. Thank the giver, thank God, and bless the funds.

I have noticed that people who have difficulty accepting money also have difficulty accepting a compliment. If you feel a lump in your throat when someone says something nice about your dress or your person, don't be dismissive of their praise by disrespecting their opinion. Simply say thank you and nothing more. Practice saying thank you until you can accept a compliment with gratitude. Compliments and money go hand in hand in the heart.

Money needs to be in a constant state of flow. It's okay to add to your savings or hold onto it for a prosperous future; just don't hold onto it out of the fear that if you spend it, it won't return.

Live in the Laws of Attraction and Circulation, and money, love, and abundance will flow continuously in your life.

Say with me and know in your heart of hearts, "I now accept love, health, harmony, and financial abundance in my life. I enjoy the flow of financial abundance in my life. I give generously, and I pay my bills, knowing money is continuously flowing into my life. I am worthy of every good thing. I am worthy of an unending stream of financial abundance. And So, It Is."

So how do we change how we think about money? We need to feel the energy of wealth and affluence.

This chapter is about abundance and the things that you can enjoy to enhance your experience on earth. If your desire is a car, a boat, a house, a vacation or anything in between, interject what you wish into your visualization and amend your affirmation to reflect your desired outcome.

Remember to only practice visualization when you are in a safe place, never while driving or operating a motorized vehicle.

Visualizations

Sit with your feet squarely on the ground. Take deep yoga breaths to calm your body and align your body with the abundance of the Universe.

As you close your eyes, imagine a beautiful tree before you. As you fully visualize this lush green tree, I want you to count the leaves. In less than a millimeter, you realize counting is an impossible task. As you contemplate this impossible undertaking, you realize the lesson is not to count the leaves but to understand the abundance, and like the tree, all you need, all you long for, is already within you.

In your visualization, you move your attention from the tree and find yourself in a very busy shopping mall. Shoppers are hurrying about with store bags; teenagers are running in and out of music stores, and families are enjoying a meal at the food court.

You begin to walk past stores and note the items in store displays that you intend on purchasing soon but continue on to a bank. Your bank.

When you arrive at the bank, you see a small welcome sign with your name on it. Several tellers smile as you walk in. You walk to the nearest representative. There is no waiting, no delay for you. She welcomes you and asks how she can help you today. You share you'd like to check your balance and make a withdrawal.

She turns her computer toward you, and you smile at the amount in your bank account. It's more than you imagined. You then tell the lady how much you want to transfer to your earthly bank account. It's okay to share all you intend to do with your funds. You tell her your intent to pay bills or do something wonderful with your funds. You now can see your bills and services paid in full.

She efficiently transfers the funds from your Universal account to your local banking account. Relief washes over you, for you are assured you now have all the funds you need.

As the transfer is completed, more money, more abundance fills your Universal banking account. You always have money when you need it. Your Universal account overflows in financial abundance.

You feel an overwhelming sense of gratitude, for you know you are a beloved child of the Universe. As you align your energy with these feelings of financial abundance, prosperity and wealth, you speak your thanks.

This or something more now manifests for you.

Mini-visualization/Daydream

When you are in a safe place and not driving or operating a motorized vehicle throughout the day, close your eyes for a mini-visualization.

In this mini-visualization, you see yourself standing on top of a small hill. The sun is shining on you. You feel the warmth and, in the warmth, you feel loved. You feel blessed.

As you watch the sky, beautiful blossoms fall toward you. I like cherry blossoms, but choose the flower you like. The flower petals fall like rain toward you until the sky is thick with beautiful flowers.

Just as they reach you, the blossoms turn to dollar bills. You extend your arms for you to realize this financial abundance is yours! All yours! There is abundance for all!

Stay in this moment until you receive the glorious joy of all your needs met.

When the mini-visualization is over, say thank you, Father-Mother-God. This or something greater now manifests in my life. And So, It Is.

Affirmations

1. I now accept love, health, harmony, and financial abundance in my life. I enjoy the flow of financial abundance in my life. I am worthy of an unending stream of financial abundance.
2. I live in a world, my world of abundance, financial good and joy. I am open, willing and grateful to accept my good in all things.
3. I enjoy the flow of financial abundance in my life. I give generously, and I pay my bills, knowing money is continuously flowing into my life. I am worthy of every good thing.
4. I am a money magnet. Everything I do turns to gold.
5. I activate the Law of Attraction, and money freely and effortlessly flows into my life.
6. I always have more money than I need. I spend my money wisely and know I have money to share, money to pay my bills and live debt-free.
7. I release any negative beliefs about money and

accept I am a child of God, worthy of every good thing to gold.

8. I now accept love, health, harmony, and financial abundance in my life. I enjoy the flow of financial abundance in my life and live in a state of well-being and prosperity.

9. I now give thanks for my new car (house, boat, etc.). I completely and fully trust the Universe to now create a new world filled with happiness, prosperity and security.

10. That which I conceive, I achieve. I am open to financial abundance!

Crystals

Citrine

The number one crystal for manifesting abundance is Citrine. For centuries it has been known as the Merchant's stone. Its vibrational energy is linked with wealth and abundance.

For many, Citrine is also used when awakening the solar plexus chakra. This beautiful crystal is one of the best stones for business and creating or attracting financial abundance or wealth.

Pyrite

Pyrite is known for its manifestation properties and is considered a powerful little crystal when manifesting financial abundance. Pyrite, which comes from the Greek word for fire, is a high-energy crystal that will help you manifest your heart's desire.

Green Jade

Green Jade is a symbol of abundance and prosperity. Green Jade has been used across many cultures and is the symbol of wealth and increased good.

Said to bring the holder good luck, Green Jade boosts energy and helps the holder-built fortune, riches and achieve success.

Suggested Talisman

Dollar sign, keychain, symbolic necklace or ring. Your talisman can even be a picture of a desired vacation or a photo of your desire good. My key chain says "Thank you Father-mother God- For my home paid in full". You can even write out a check to yourself for the amount of money you desire.

Your talisman can be anything that represents your desire.

CHAPTER 10 CAREER, EMPLOYMENT

My friends have marveled at how easily it always seems for me to find a high-paying job. I am not bragging nor have a special potion or spell; I just know how to use the Law of Attraction when seeking jobs. I am going to now share this technique with you.

Before I do, I want to share my experience with an employer who loved my resume but said he was going on a three-week vacation and wanted for me to wait until he and his wife had returned.

The job was great, I liked the employer, but I could not afford to wait three weeks before I started receiving a paycheck.

When I returned home, instead of deep diving into victimhood or going into frantic worry, I turned to prayer. With my prayer journal, I went outside and began by contemplating the abundance of the Universe. In meditation, I visualized how this job or something better would manifest for me. I saw myself working at this company or at a similar position with a different business in a detailed imagery.

I spent a few moments elevating my energy to align with this position. I allowed the happiness of having this job to bubble up inside me, filling me with happiness.   In my visualization, I saw myself working in my new role, collaborating with the art department and various heads of the creative departments. I saw myself delivering the products to my clients and receiving rave reviews and appreciation from my clients. I saw myself happily spending the money I earned as I met my obligations and enjoying my life. When I peaked in my prosperity consciousness, I turned this over to the Law of Attraction and allowed this Law to works its magic in my life.

As I released my prayer, I was completely open to any position and completely open to my highest good. I ceased all worry and just let go with the assertion, this or something better now manifests for me.

It was about 20 minutes later when the employer called me back and said, "Why wait? My staff can bring you up to date on the accounts, and when I return from my vacation, we'll hit the ground running."

Always end your prayer or affirmation with, this or something better now manifests for me. Don't bind the Universe with a limited outcome, be open to extraordinary opportunities.

You see a particular job as your only choice, your only hope, you limit the good the Universe has planned for you. The Universe sees far more and may deliver a better position with a greater salary.

There is no special secret sauce as you begin your manifestation work. State your desire or intention. Remember that which you are seeking is also seeking you.

There is a wonderful African proverb that says: "When you pray, move your feet."

With a background of over 40 years in international marketing, I want to share with you some marketing tips to help you acquire your ideal job.

Attracting the Job You Want

With an intention or desire in mind, you set into motion the Laws of Attraction. You lay the foundation by writing down every detail you want in your new position. No desire or wish is too small. Your manifest list of details should include everything you want your ideal job to offer.

What is important to you? Write down a realistic salary that not only pays your bills but gives you extra income to more fully enjoy your life.

Be realistic. Unless you are mentally and internally aligned with a $ 75,000 annual salary and are prepared to do the work that the salary range requires, I suggest you write down a yearly income you can align with now. You have to be mentally and spiritually aligned with your annual income and know you are worth it.

If your last job paid you $20,000 a year, be open to accepting $30,000 to $35,000. You can always increase your salary at a later time!

What benefits are you looking for in your new position? Do you want this new job to offer insurance, education, gym memberships? I am always pleased when coffee and snacks are available in the break room.

Is it important that you work with a company with integrity and supports the community with events like food drives or having a toy donation box at the holidays?

Do you want to work from home or be close to home?

Do you want a flexible schedule, or a position that will allow you to work from home when your child is not well?

I think I am speaking for everyone when I say you want to be respected by your supervisors and co-workers and spend your time in a worker-friendly environment.

Your salary should cover your bills but allow you to have extra money for enjoying movies, a night out with friends and a life that gives you a reason to celebrate.

What are your preferred hours, 9 AM to 5 PM or another schedule? Do you prefer a thirty-minute or sixty-minute lunch?

Do you prefer a company that is stable and offers you room to grow?

Write down whatever you desire w and focus on it.

Use my deal point, break point suggestion technique when you hear the company's offer. Decide what a deal point is and what is a definite break point. For instance, your job may offer you everything you desire but insists all employees take a sixty-minute lunch. For me, that would be a deal point and acceptable. Would it work for you?

A break point for me would be if smoking is allowed in your work space. That would be a break point for me as I don't want to be around smokers. Smokers are not bad people; I just don't want to be around smoke. What are deal points and break points for you?

Be as clear with intention as possible. Before putting all this together, I want to add a few real-world marketing tips to help you clinch that job.

Employment Marketing Tips

First, check and double-check your resume. Does it need updating? Is everything spell-checked?

While you are at it, update your LinkedIn profile. If you don't have one, create a LinkedIn profile with a business headshot. LinkedIn has fantastic jobs on its career page. You will also find a wonderful group of Headhunters/job recruiters on LinkedIn.

While on LinkedIn, review any companies you are interested in and follow those companies for information to help you secure a job. Look up the company's Human Resource Director and write a short note like, I wanted to reach out to you and then explain why you would be a good fit. This note should be short and professional. Save your resume and personal details for a live interview.

Take a look at your posts on all social media. While you are job hunting, you might want to think twice about posting unflattering comments or photos. I can assure you the Human Resources recruiters are looking at social media profiles more than ever. Have fun on social media but remember recruiters decide if you are a good fit for their companies based on what they find on your social media pages.

Research companies close to you, set your criteria. Don't rely just on job posting sites. Go to companies you desire to work at and post directly at the company site under career opportunities.

Before you apply or have an interview, make sure you have looked at the company website. When you are interviewed, you will impress your recruiter with your knowledge about the company and your position there. People or, in this case companies will only care about you if you show you care about them.

If you are interviewing with a Recruiter and education comes up, with the knowledge you learned about the recruiter from the company's profile; you can ask, how did you like the University of Central Florida? Again, this is yet another way to demonstrate you took the time to research the company and once again be impressed by you!

If the Recruiter or interviewer doesn't ask what you know about the company, be sure you interject it into your conversation. You might say something like, "I see your company does a food drive every year. I appreciate a company that gives back to the community. It's something I would love to participate in." Watch the interviewers' eyes flash as they recognize you have done your homework.

First impressions count, so arrive ahead of your appointment time and dress for success.

If you know someone who works at the company, mention that Suzie says this is a great company, but of course, leave out any negative comments Suzie might have shared.

Create a Benefit Analysis Sheet. A Benefit Analysis Sheet brings your skills and work history in line with the position you are looking for. A Benefit Analysis sheet makes the interviews job easier for you and the recruiter.

My Benefit Analysis sheet says, I have a strong track record as a New Business Development Specialist with the ability to generate leads, develop referrals through prospecting, cold calling and as well as taking full advantage of networking events.

The next line says Linn Random is an extremely strong communicator with strong written and verbal skills and the ability to work with many personalities.

Try to connect to the interviewer as the interview starts. For instance, if you see a picture of a dog, tell them about your dog or children, or if you see Napoleon Hills' book on *Think and Grow Rich*, you can mention it's one of your favorites also. Be genuine, of course, don't say you love cats if you are allergic to them. Don't share you like Napoleon Hill if you are not prepared with a favorite passage from his book. The truth always comes out.

At your interview, be prepared. Do a google search on responding to tough questions.

For example, when asked what is my biggest weakness. I say something like, "I'm a perfectionist. It's important to me that I get my work right the first time. I really get annoyed with myself if I turn in something that is not up to standards."

Here are another one of those annoying questions, where do you see yourself in five years? Your answer could be, I would like to think my hard work will afford me greater responsibility, and I anticipate being an expert in my role."

Don't worry about sounding too cheeky. The recruiter will appreciate your response. For more ideas, type in tough interview questions and go through the questions and responses that are natural to you.

If the interviewer asks you about salary, ask them what are the parameters of this position? Let them answer first.

One last tip, I always have a thank you card for the interviewer and pass it to the receptionist after I leave the interview or if you prefer, send the interviewer a thank-you email when you get home. Thanking someone for their time is always good form.

As you drive to a job interview, think this is my way to work, then this is where I park. As you pass convivence stores, affirm this is where I pick up snacks or get gas.

When you want into the company, think this is the front entrance to my job.

Before and after, see yourself working there, depositing

a big paycheck, being praised by a supervisor. Make your visualization as detailed as possible.

The following is a visualization for a generic job. Amend the following visualization and affirmation for a specific position you desire. Always add, this or something better now manifests for you.

Generic Job Interview Visualization

Sit with your feet squarely on the ground. Take deep yoga breaths to calm your body and align your body with the energy of abundance and service.

As you close your eyes, you allow the calm energy of peace and love to rise within you, filling every cell of your body with love.

See yourself in a company's reception area. Other applicants are there and waiting politely. You are well prepared and have practiced the interview questions you anticipate you will be asked. You are confident and assured of this job.

The human resources or owner of the company comes into the waiting area and invites you into a small conference room.

After a bit of small talk, you feel comfortable and assured you will be getting this job.

The interviewer asks you questions and is clearly pleased with your answers. As he tells you about his company, you smile, for this position is exactly what you are looking for.

The interviewer now takes you for a tour of the building, pointing out managers and staff. People smile at you as you pass. You realize how welcoming and supportive your fellow employees will be.

You are shown your desk, the breakroom and the outside picnic area. You are asked to fill out employee paperwork or complete the form online for onboarding.

You see yourself easily completing your tasks and duties. You follow directions and help others. Your managers see you helping others and later tell you what a value you are to the company.

You see yourself obtaining a very positive review where the employer compliments you on your production and positive, dedicated attitude.

Your paycheck is deposited, and you see yourself enjoying life. You take vacations, easily afford your home and drive the auto that you love.

You see yourself getting or receiving an award at work at everyone and thoroughly enjoy the cheers and applause you receive.

You have never been happier in your life and see your life improving every day in every way.

Finish by affirming, in faith, "This or something better now manifests for you. And So, It Is!"

Affirmations

1. I speak my word for a job close to home, where I am valued and appreciated by coworkers and supervisors.
2. There is no delay in the divine plan for me. My desire to work and be of service is my prayer answered.
3. I am grateful for the job offered to me. I give thanks my job pays more than I imagined.
4. As a child of God, I now give thanks as I manifest the perfect employment for me.
5. I am worthy of the fantastic job I desire. I am led to the right job, at the right salary, at the right location for the highest good of my experience.
6. I move forward in confidence and assurance that I have the right job for me.
7. I am open to experience my dream job with the salary I desire to easily support my lifestyle and my needs and my family's needs.
8. Thank you, Father-Mother-God, for my new job now.
9. I trust the Universe to bring me and my new job together
10. I am fulfilled and grateful for my job now. My work is God's work, as I serve God, I benefit others.

Crystals

There are many wonderful crystals to aid you in securing a job. I am listing several crystals to assist you in a job interview or perhaps on a sales call for your business.

Job Manifestation

As previously mentioned, Pyrite is a crystal of manifestation. Citrine for money and wealth. Rose Quartz and Clear Quartz will assist you in communication and connection for a job interview.

Green Aventurine also helps open the door for new opportunities, offers you good luck in job interviews, and embraces confidence and leadership qualities. Green Adventure is one of my favorite healing crystals and will help enhances creativity, confidence and increase connections in the workplace. Green Aventurine is called the stone of opportunity and is said to be the luckiest of all crystals.

Green Aventurine is another crystal to help and balance the Heart Chakra.

Crystals to aid in Communication

Lapis lazuli is a bluestone used to promote communication, stimulates self-expression and mental clarity.

Turquoise and Aquamarine are great stones to help you keep you in organizing your thoughts for clarity and will help you communicate.

Sodalite is a beautiful crystal that aids in communication and helps us think calmly and rationally

Blue Sapphire is another good crystal to help you support your throat chakra and your communication skills.

Crystals for Balance and Calming

If you need help with balance or calming, use Black Tourmaline Celestite. Fluorite and beautiful Tiger's Eye.

CHAPTER 11 HEAL
THE PLANET

It is our privilege, pleasure and responsibility to call this planet home.

I think everyone reading this book recognizes that our beautiful planet needs our prayers.

In September 2020, the World Health Organization published a report that stated 9 out of 10 people live in countries with excessive air pollution.

The Amazon Rainforests are some of the world's Earth's oldest ecosystems, and they are quite literally the world's lungs. We breathe in oxygen and breathe out carbon dioxide. Trees take in the carbon dioxide, and in return, create the oxygen. This process is called photosynthesis and is vital to all life on earth.

By 2050, scientists say by 2050 there will be more plastic in the ocean than fish. Our rivers, streams, lakes, and oceans are polluted daily with toxic chemicals and biological agents.

Precious and rare animal species are becoming endangered. Without our help, many will become extinct; future generations will see these precious animals only in museums, movies and photographs. They will ask, why didn't we help when we could have made a difference.

Humans are the cause, but we can also be the solution.

I urge everyone reading this book to participate in change. Create a personal action plan.

We can each do our part by recycling, converting our garbage to compost for our gardens and plants. Help our beautiful animals survive by donating to charitable organizations that help species survive.

If you dine out, bring your own reusable doggie bag container. Instead of plastic forks, bring your own utensils, coffee cups and drink containers.

Conserve electricity by using natural light. Replace traditional Light Bulbs with LED lighting. Identify and unplug energy vampires. Conserve water.

Volunteer for cleanups in your community and help others understand the importance and value of our natural resources.

Plant a tree and use non-toxic chemicals in the home and office.

Each of us can participate. Together we can save this planet.

We can also save the world by lifting our vibrational energy, and by doing so, we join with others and together, we can effect change.

Vibrational Energy

For centuries, humans have noticed behavioral changes during full moons. Scientists will refute this as fiction but can't explain the rise in crime, increased emergency room activity and erratic sleep patterns people have during these periods.

And why not, we are made up of water, and like the tides, our bodies are affected by the moon.

Seasonal changes and world events also effect us. Positive events uplift us. Negative events such as catastrophic losses of life impacts us negatively.

We have within us the power to raise not only our vibrational energy but collectively, as we join with others, our combined vibrational energy lifts the planet's frequency and vibration. We do this when we meditate, think positive thoughts and words, and express tolerance and kindness toward our fellow man.

We can also increase our vibration levels by eating high vibration food such as fruits and vegetables. Alcohol is a depressant that, once past the initial temporary euphoric effect, will lower our vibration.

Just as we stop polluting the environment, it's important to eliminate toxins from our bodies. You can affect your own health, your moods, feelings and well-being by eating healthy. We have the power to change our lives. We have the power to change the world. We are our own miniature Universe.

As a tiny pebble falls into the center of a pond, it sends out a circular vibrational ring that spreads and grows until it reaches the water's edge. You do the same with your vibrational energy. The energy and emotions you feel stretch across our galaxy to the far reaches of the Universe.

Your thoughts matter. You matter. You hold within you the vibrational power to change the Universe.

You achieve this through meditation, when you think good thoughts and speak divine words of love and peace. When you are feeling low, you pull down your energy, and you impact the planet. However, when you feel joy, radiate love, you lift not only yourself but the world.

In our busy, bustling modern society, many people have forgotten how to breathe. They take short and oftentimes shallow breaths that never quite fill up our lungs to full capacity. Have you ever watched a baby sleep? Their little tummies rise and fall in their sleep because they are practicing "diaphragmatic breathing," referred to as "belly breathing."

When we take deep breaths, we realign our vibrational energy, and in doing so, it calms us, soothes and relaxes us. As our vibration energy fills us, we unwind, and in this relaxed state, we send out peace and tranquility to the world.

Yoga combines the benefits of breathing, meditation, and brings our bodies in sync with the rhythmic movement and flow of the earth. Yoga has been shown to improve blood sugar levels, gentle exercise to improve strength, relieve painful conditions and alleviate symptoms of anxiety and depression.

In yoga, you learn to breathe to the count of 8, holding your breath to the count of 3, and slowly releasing your breath to the count of 8. I recommend, if you do yoga breaths, to visualize bringing in golden light with each breath. As you hold the breath within you, see this golden light swirl about your body, gathering tension and anxiety and then slowly release the tension and any negative feelings when you breathe out.

I practice yoga and can attest to the benefits of improved strengh, eleavation of painful conditions and balance.

Meditation and breathwork can positively affect your blood pressure; they can affect your mood and elevate your vibrational energy.

Strolling thru a city park is a great way to raise your vibration, for as you watch young lovers or older lovers hold hands, you can feel their love. As you take in squirrels scampering about, or get perfectly lost in the sparkle of sunlight dancing across a canopy of trees, you draw in the peace and flow of nature, and as you do, you become relaxed and refreshed, enjoying the simple pleasure of fresh air.

A favorite ritual of mine is to go barefoot outside and rub the bottom of my feet into the ground as I let Mother Giai recharge me with her energy flow. In fact, refresh yourself in nature, whenever possible, if only it's a few moments a day.

Sunlight brings with it much-needed Vitamin D to us, and medical preofessionals recommend 15 minutes a day of sunlight. So too gentle rains soothe the soul and lull us into a beautiful afternoon sleep.

Music affects our vibrational and can stimulate our senses with thoughts and images of love, peace, and harmony. Music uplifts our spirits and our frequencies. Music therapy heals our souls. The vibrational ringing of bells reaches deep within us, and positivity impacts us. One of my favorite videos was a man who played his piano for elephants. The elephants gathered around the old man and enjoyed the music he played.

We are the world. We are the earth's children. We can heal our planet through recycling, and reusing. We can lift planetary vibration through our thoughts of love.

You are important. You are needed. You are cherished.

You are changing the world.

Visualizations

Sit with your feet squarely on the ground. Take deep yoga breaths to calm and align your body with the earth's energy.

As you close your eyes, you are aware of a deep and beautiful peace deep within you. You allow this blissful energy to fill every cell, every part of your body, with love. As this beautiful feeling grows within you, you feel as silverly glistening roots shoot out from your feet and extend down into the earth, where they wrap around a beautiful golden core. Feeling safe and secure, you see your energy flow back to your body.

As you return to the earth's surface, you open your mind's eye you find yourself in a deep green forest. You are standing in a small clearing with a canopy of trees above you. The air is cool to your skin and feels comfortable, part of nature. You catch the soft fragrance of wildflowers in the air carried by a gentle wind that caresses your face. You are safe, sheltered and protected.

As you look about you, you watch as shimmering streams of golden light slip through the green canopy to the forest floor. With the light brightening the forest world, you watch as a doe looks appears before you. She pauses to watch you then disappears into the woods. She knows you are here to help her and her kind.

Three small rabbits scamper in front of you, and you are suddenly aware of the sounds of birds chirping in the trees and the occasional dark flutter of a bird crossing through the light.

You notice a path is before you, and you begin to walk down that trail. As you walk along, you see you are traveling next to a beautiful stream and flows around rocks. The water is so clear, and you see fish darting in and about the water's edge. The water sparkles as sunlight shimmers. You are keenly aware of the fresh scent of the stream.

As you continue walking, the forest gives way to tall grasses, and you follow the path to a sandy dune. Reaching the top of the dune, you happily discover a long sandy beach.

You walk down to the beach and smell the heady scent of the sea. In the distance, you watch as seagulls glide across the top of white foamy waves. You watch as erns scamper around the shoreline, and an occasional small crab digs a hole into the sand and disappears beneath it. The sand feels crunching beneath your feet.

You look down and find yourself in a beautiful short greco-roman dress and walk into the sea, allowing the water to dance playfully around your feet. The water is warm and inviting, and you walk into the sea. When it's up to your chest, you dive. In this realm, you can swim, and enjoy the water world around you.

As you swim, you can feel all the negative thoughts, cares of the world, all concerns, just float away from you. Dolphins join you, and if you wish, you can grab a fin or ride the back of them

As you return to shore, you stand and open your arms and let the sun bathe you.

In peace and in power, you allow your loving energy to flow from you to bathe the beach and the world in your healing light. As your healing energy expands across the sea and the land, it eliminates pollutions, chemicals and plastics, you realize your power is making the oceans healthy and teeming with fish.

Your energy cleans the streams, releases elements and polutants from the earth and restores the plane to health.

Rise above our planet and see it beautiful, healthy and with love and peace.

You now envision world peace, and so it is as you watch leaders of countries come together. Children are fed, everyone is loved, and your kindness is so powerful that the earth is restored.

Allow yourself a moment to feel what you have done this day and be grateful for this planet and your part in healing it.

Slowly, you open your eyes and are assured of your visualization. Your word, your loving energy, has transformed the earth into a more peaceful and beautiful place.

And So It is.

Spend a few moments each day and visualize a beautiful ocean teeming with fish. Clean flowing streams. Beautiful mountains manganate filled with trees, forest animals. Green jungles and savannahs filled with animal populations. Visualize our cities, our planet with clean air and our rivers with pollution-free water.

Rise above our planet and see it beautiful, healthy and with love and peace.

Affirmations

1. Today more than ever before, I do my part to create a healthy world. I recognize myself as an important part of this change. And so it is.
2. I give thanks for my beautiful, healthy, perfect planet.
3. As I speak my word for peace and goodwill to all men, women, and children of this planet, my loving thoughts bring world harmony to all nations and people.
4. As I speak my word for clean streams and clean air, my loving energy spreads across the planet and makes the water pure and the planet whole and refreshed.
5. I give thanks for restoration and an abundance of wildlife.
6. Every time I eat good food, drink water, I give thanks for my good, and as I do so, my attitude of gratitude blesses the waters, renews the land and all who walk upon it.
7. At the core of my being, there is an infinite well of love. As I send this love, my love across the globe, my loving energy touches the heart and minds of every

man, woman and child in this world.

8. My thoughts of a peaceful planet are answered. My thoughts of health and abundance create health and abundance of all, for all.
9. I now visualize my love and peace circulating the planet. Wars stop, children and animals are loved, this planet experiences a renaissance of life.
10. As I send out love to all the earth, all creatures great and small experience peace and a bounty of love and kindness.

Crystals to Heal the Planet

Brown Aragonite

Aragonite is a dedicated healer who is intensely bonded with the earth's vibrational energy. There are four varieties of Aragonite white, blue, lilac and brown. Respectfully, lilac and blue raise the earth's vibrations. White purifies earth's power, and brown stabilizes our world and supports overall planetary healing.

Like Black Tourmaline, Aragonite is good for grounding. Many use this stone when working with the root chakra.

Herkimer Diamonds

Discovered in Herkimer, New York, Herkimer Diamonds are not real diamonds but are treasured due to their dazzling clarity. Herkimer diamonds are brighter than their clear quartz and have a geometrical shape. Herkimer Diamonds possess very high vibration energy and are known as the stone of attunement.

Herkimer Diamonds are associated with planetary root healing and aid in both the physical and spiritual worlds. They help in the elimination of planetary stress.

Smokey Quartz

Another crystal to assist you in prayers for our planet is the Smokey Quartz.   Found around the world, the Smokey Quartz absorbs negative energies and stimulates earth healing as well as aiding the planetary vibration.

The Smokey Quartz can be found around the world and was a favorite used by the Druids. Known as the Stone of Power, the Smokey Quartz has been used in tribal ceremonies and in shamanistic rituals for centuries.

Fairy Amethyst

Fairy Amethyst, known as the Spirit Quartz, is a high-vibrational earth energy crystal that can be used during mediation and can help in planetary healing and strengthen a connection to fairies.

Appreciated for its soft lavender color, the Fairy Amethyst aids in removing environmental pollutants and stabilizing the earth. This very pretty crystal stretches into fairy kingdoms and across multi-dimensional realms.

The Fairy Amethyst crystal works can be used in cleansing all chakras.

CHAPTER 13 CONCLUSION

I hope you have enjoyed this book. I wrote it because I have successfully manifested many things in my life. Necessary things and things and dreams which brought me great pleasure and personal fulfillment.

I wrote this book because I want to share my successes with you, and I want you to have all that you desire.

As I began this work, I was well aware of the many books on the Law of Attraction. I found many books that explained the Law of Attraction but few that made the connection between what you desire and how to align it with your good.

The secret to the Law of Attraction is in the details. Those details include aligning your energy with the Laws of Vibrations, Correspondence and feelings of worthiness and acceptance. All these laws must come into alignment for your manifest dream to be achieved.

Saying an affirmation doesn't work, unless you believe it. Aligning your energy with that which you desire will bring your desire to fruition.

One last word of caution, the elements in this book will only work if you apply them daily to your life. I, too, dearest reader, have hundreds of books on prosperity and abundance, but it's only when I use the tools do my manifest dreams become a reality.

Some of your manifestations will occur instantly. Others will take a moment in time. It depends on you and aligning your energy and frequency.

Like love, manifestation is an inside job. You make your magic happen!

The Law of Attraction works with other laws like the

Law of Vibration, the Law of Cause and Effect and the Law of Correspondence. All these laws must come into alignment for your desire to work.

As I close this book, I have included a recommended books and resources to expand on your journey, along with a chapter on my book *Reincarnation Journey of the Soul*.

Again, thank you very much for reading my book. I appreciate it so much and would appreciate a kind review after you have read it.

Whatever you dream about, it will all be yours if you claim it.

Know that I will be in your front row clapping!

Author's Note to You

You are invited to a free chapter read of my book, *Reincarnation Journey of the Soul* at the end of this boo and a chapter on my book on Cord Cutting.

I hope you enjoyed this book and you manifest all your dreams!

MANIFESTATION THRU

Visualization & Affirmation Workbook (c)

Linn Random

Manifestation Workbook

Jessica Wallace King

CHAPTER 1 LAW OF ATTRACTION- KNOWLEDGE ASSESSMENT

I know the Law of Attraction works because I have consistently demonstrated the Law of Attraction in my life. I manifested the perfect man for me, my husband of 22 years. I have manifested my home and have co-created prosperity in my life.

When this book was first published, it did not have this workbook. I have added the workbook to help you assess your understanding of the Law of Attraction and how to put your knowledge into practical application. If you put in the effort, you will manifest your desired outcome.

However, you must release all negative thoughts of yourself and other and be fully open to your good.

Know, the Universe is always working for your highest good. Don't outline. Be fully open. Keep in mind, if you fail to get a specific job, a home or a particular person, be glad because the Universe has someone or better for you waiting in the wings.

There is no course grade or certificate for completing the workbook section. This workbook is for your personal use. There is no need to share your information with anyone unless you work with a private counselor like Jessica Wallace King.

Since first published, I have received astonishing feedback from readers around the world who have shared their successes. From improved health, to new careers, finding a life partner as well as the manifestation of things such as cars, homes, vacations or new computers, practitioners of the Law of Attraction have successfully brought their desires from the ethereal plane to the manifest plane.

These people are not unique or have extraordinary abilities. They just took the time and put in the effort to make their magic happen. You can too.

Please note, this book will only work in accordance with your belief, and your energy alignment with the thing you desire. It's important to align your mental equivalent and remove any internal blockages or negative beliefs.

The first few questions are offered to assess your understanding of the Law of Attraction.

Keep in mind, this book in no way a substitute for medical advice. The author, publisher or any third party associated with this book are not responsible for any loss, claim or damage arising out of the use or misuse of the suggestions. The intent of the author is only to offer information of a general nature and guidelines to help you in your quest for emotional and spiritual wellbeing.

While you can certainly work simultaneously on as many desires as you like, I recommend, especially if you are new to the manifestation process, to select that which you desire most. After you successfully mastered the Law of Attraction, future manifestations for anything will becomes easier.

So, in your own words, consider your thoughts, beliefs and how the Law of Attraction will work in your life.

There is no time limit, this workbook is to help you manifest that which you desire from the ethereal plane to the manifest plane.

You can fill in the blanks but if you need more space, write it out in a notebook or word document.

Knowledge Assessment

Explain the Law of Attraction

_____

_____

_____

Explain the Law of Correspondence

_____

_____

_____

Explain the Law of Circulation

_____

_____

_____

_____

Explain Three Type of Invisible Laws we can assess every day

_____

_____

_____

_____

What is holding you back?

_____

_____

_____

What are your beliefs about Money?

_____

_____

_____

Do I feel unworthy of that which I desire?

_____

_____

_____

Do I judge others or myself?

_____

_____

_____

_____

Do I hate anyone? Myself, others, a relative, neighbor, political figure or group?

_____

_____

_____

_____

What am I willing to release, in order to accept my good? This includes all negative thoughts about others or myself? Identify and release these blockages.

_____

_____

_____

_____

_____

_____

_____

_____

What self-limiting or negative thoughts am I holding onto to? (You are too old, too young? Etc.)

_____

_____

_____

_____

I now let go of any negative or all self-limiting beliefs?

_____

_____

_____

_____

—————————————————————————————————————

———————————————————

Explain Energy Alignment.

I go into a meditative state and feel a tiny pearl of joy bubble up from deep inside of me. I let this effervesce of joy fill me until I am fully consumed by incredible happiness, knowing, truly knowing, I now possess the thing which I desire.
Write out how you intend to align your energy with your desire.

————————————————————————————————————
————————————————————————————————————
————————————————————————————————————
————————————————————————————————————
————————————————————————————————————
————————————————————————————————————

———————

The dream which I now choose to bring into my manifest plane is:

————————————————————————————————————
————————————————————————————————————
————————————————————————————————————
————————————————————————————————————
————————————————————————————————————

———————————————————

Let's do a quick review on the steps on how to do a visualization and manifest your dream.

How to Visualize
1. Have a clear picture in your mind of your Desire.
2. State your Intention with Energy behind each word.
3. Prepare yourself by grounding, meditating, and connecting to

the Universe.

4. Align your emotional energy with that that you desire. Let it completely fill you.

5. Visualize your Desired Outcome with heartfelt passion, Infuse your visualization with as many details as possible.

6. End your Visualization with an overwhelming sense and feeling of gratitude and say, "This or something better manifests for me now!"

7. Release your Desire to the Universe assured God, the Universe, answers prayer.

8. Close your visualization by saying, "Amen" or "And So It is!"

At the beginning of each chapter, I suggest crystals and a talisman. Neither are necessary, but I find them to be helpful in keeping my mind focused and my energy elevated throughout the day.

Crystals help us fine tune our energy with the visualization and manifestation process.

Talisman or amulets serve the same purpose. Their purpose is to keep your mind and energy focused on your desire.

As you touch your crystal or talisman, and say an affirmation, your energy will receive a boost to reinforce that which you desire into the manifest plane.

I find crystals and talismans effective for me as they help me make my dream appear much faster and besides, they are fun!

CHAPTER 2 HEALTH

Recommended Crystals
Clean quartz, green aventurine and malachite.
Select a crystal of your choice and hold it while you meditate. When working with crystals, I use two crystals; one for each palm. The crystals you select can be raw or polished.

Suggested Talisman.
Your talisman can be a small notebook filled with affirmations, a keychain with a sport's charm, or something that reminds you of your health goal. As you notice your talisman throughout the day, remind yourself of your desire and use it to keep your energy high and your mind focused on your desire.

You need not share your talisman, crystal or desire with anyone. In fact, keeping it in silence can build up the pressure to help you manifest. If you do want to share your goal with a friend, make sure you only speak about it to people who will support you.

Health
I was introduced to metaphysical healing through the teachings of the Church of Religious Science. This church was founded by Ernest Holmes, recognized as one of the founders of the new thought movement. His book, The Science of Mind shows readers how to change their lives and improve their health by positive prayer, called treatment work and believing in positive affirmations. His book, *The Science of Mind,* has been in continuous print since 1926.

Since the publication of *The Science of Mind*, numerous books have been written to include *The Power of Positive*

Thinking by Dr. Norman Vincent Peal and books by Dr. Joseph Murphy and Catherine Ponder.

The premise of these books is to align your energy and thoughts with your desires.

Louise Hay wrote a powerful book titled, *You Can Heal Your Life.* In her book, she wrote about her experiences in healing and how by using the power of the mind, she transformed her life. If you don't own this book, I urge you to purchase a copy.

In these books any others like them, you will read about the correlation between the mind and body experience.

Both Hay and Holmes share a metaphysical causation bought on by thoughts about the self. For instance, back and should pain can be caused by feelings of lack of emotional support.

In my own experience, if I have a headache, I will take an aspirin but look inside myself for any fear, confusion, or stress in my life that might be the cause of the headache. After taking my medication, I begin doing a meditation and affirming peace in my life.

As I am not a medical professional, I refer you to Ernest Holmes and Louise Hay for study and research to help you identify the personal support you may wish to add to your diagnosis.

In this section, I am only offering a general visualization and affirmation and refer you to Louise Hay or Ernest Holmes to help you identify illness or disease and the mental causation behind them.

I always suggest you discuss with your physician before you engage in any holistic practice to ensure your choice is safe and will aid you in your healing practices.

General Visualization

1. Begin with grounding yourself.
2. Relax your body with yoga breaths.

3. From deep within you become aware of a bright light within you and you recognize it as your own divinity and the divine connection to the God within you.

4. In your visualization go to your sacred place. Your sacred place may be the Healing Temple of Archangel Raphael, a beach, a mountain top or in a grassy pasture.

5. In your visualization, see a healing green or white healing light comes down from the heavens. It bathes you in its beautiful healing light.

6. Stay in the visualization until you feel fullyhealed.

7. Offer thanks to God for your healing and release your mediation in peace.

Do this meditation as many times throughout the day and you can and use your affirmations to support your mediation.

You will find numerous healing meditations, visualizations are available to you on CD, books, and on YouTube. Find one that works for you.

General Affirmations for Health

1. I am whole, healthy, perfect and complete.

2. I embrace health, I live a healthy lifestyle.

3. I release any and all negative thoughts. I am fully open to the healing energy of God.

4. Perfect health is my birthright.

5. I give thanks to the Universe, for my radiant health. God's healing energy flows through my body in loving good health.

6. I eat only healthy foods, think only positive thoughts and lovingly treat my body with
exquisite self-care.

7.I am healthy, strong, whole and complete. I am open and receptive to all the healing   energies in the Universe.

8. I love and honor myself by maintaining good health, every day

in every way.

9. I release any thoughts that tell me I am unworthy of good health, I embrace good health, love and enjoy my healthy lifestyle.

10.Thank you, Father-Mother-God, for my good health.

CHAPTER 3 MANIFESTING A LOVING PARTNER

Recommended Crystals
Rose Quartz, Rhodochrosite, Moonstone.

Suggested Talisman
Your talisman can be any small trinket or item that is a touchstone to keep your mind and emotions focused on manifesting a loving partner.

My preferred talisman for romance is a heart-shaped locket. If you use a locket, put a small picture of your ideal match on the inside or perhaps a couple in a wedding photo. Remember do not outline for a specific someone.

As you move through your day, when you see or touch your locket perhaps during a business meeting or at a red light while you are driving, you are boosting your energy and bringing your energy into alignment with your desire. No one is the wiser.

A ring, bracelet, or piece of jewelry work as well so keep your vision on the prize that awaits you and allow the power of love fill you.

Attracting Love
.

Let's explore your beliefs to make sure you are in the right mindset for a perfect union. Keep in mind, like attracts like, if you are needy, you will attract someone who will make you feed needy or is needy himself. If feel you are somehow unworthy of your good, the Universe will bring you someone who will reinforce your sense of worthiness.

When you love yourself, you will attract Mr. Right, not Mr. Right now. Like attracts like, so if you feel unworthy, you will surely attract someone who will mistreat you.

Remember, before you can bring someone who will love you and treasure you, you must first fully love yourself.

Questions
Do I believe myself to be worthy of a fabulous relationship where I am loved, treasured and respected?

_____
_____
_____
_____

What activities do you do during the day to let the Universe know you love and appreciate yourself?

_____
_____
_____
_____

Make a list of traits and characteristics you love about yourself. I'll start you off.

I have a great smile.   I have a good heart.
I am a great friend.   I am kind to animals
I am a supportive, loving companion.   I am loyal.
I am very smart and super funny.   I deserve love.

Continue adding to your list until you can look at yourself through my eyes. I see a beautiful loving person who is worthy of a companion who will treat her with love and respect. You are so worthy of this great love; remember God would never give your heart a desire without also giving you the answer.

Now write your list:

_____

_____

_____

_____

_____

_____

_____

_____

_____

_____

_____

_____

_____

_____

_____

_____

_____

_____

_____

_____

_____

_____

_____

_____

_____

_____

_____

_____

_____

_____

Wow, looking at your list you have to agree with me, you are a wonderful person! You do most certainly deserve the love you desire!

`   Now let's write down all the personality traits, attributes, YOU want in an ideal partner.

Traits and Attributes I want in a Partner

_____

_____

_____

_____

_____

_____

_____

_____

_____

_____

_____

_____

_____

_____

_____

_____

_____

_____

_____

_____

_____

_____

_____

Your ideal your partner will be what you request so be specific. In my list 22 years ago, I wrote down I wanted a partner who enjoyed fishing and an outdoor lifestyle.

When I met my husband, he literally checked just about all my brackets. However, I realized I had not been specific about fishing. What I wanted was a partner who enjoyed the outdoors, but not so much it consumed the entire weekend, dawn to dusk. I was in love, so I chose to be flexible if a partner. Deal point, break point.

So, if you neglect to be specific, be prepared to follow your deal point, break point compromises. For instance, deal point, he loves golf or football and will spend part of his weekend relaxing with his interests. You are not a football fan but as willing to enjoy game time with him or will use that free time to relax with your friends.

Breakpoint, he was abusive in his last relationship or has an ongoing substance abuse problem. If you see a problem, no matter how handsome he is or how much money he has, don't compromise your values or ideals.

Visualization and Daydreams

Spend a couple of minutes throughout the day or before sleep visualize or day dream about your ideal partner. In this instance, it's okay to daydream about activities and fun you want to share with him or her.

What is your favorite restaurant?

_____
_____
_____
_____
_____
_____

What do you and your partner do on Sundays?

_____
_____
_____
_____

What are your weekday routines?

_____
_____
_____

What are your weekend routines?

_____

_____

_____

_____

Where will you spend your vacations?

_____

_____

_____

_____

Where will you get married? Who will be there?

_____

_____

_____

_____

_____

See yourself and your partner goals in the next 3 years, 5 years, 10 years?

_____

_____

Will you have children?

_____

_____

What do you do on special date nights?

_____

_____

_____

_____

Do you like nature walks, hiking, sports or movies, museums or enjoy your happiness at home?

_____

_____

_____

_____

Where will the two of you live? apartment, home, beach, forest, suburbs, city?

_____

_____

_____

_____

It's okay to spend time daydreaming as you breathe in joy and love into your visualizations.

Remember, do not get lost in your daydreams or visualization while operating heavy machinery or driving a car. Enjoy your daydreams or visualize only when it's safe to do so.

Affirmations

1. I now activate the Law of Attraction, knowing I am worthy of a loving perfect companion for me. I am open to giving and receiving love.

2. I trust the Universe to bring into my experience a loving and kind companion into my life today.

3. I am worthy of a beautiful loving companion and a beautiful life.

4. I am open to a beautiful loving relationship where I am loved, appreciated, treasured.

5. I now tighten the magical connection between me and my true love. I am in the right place at the right time to meet my partner. There is no delay in the Divine Plan for me.

6. I now connect to my perfect companion. My loving relationship is more than I can ever imagine.

7. I release the past and let love flow into my life. I am open to a new experience of more love, more joy, more kindness and more happiness than I have ever imagined. And so, it is.

8. I radiate with love. The more I love, the more loving thoughts, the closer my perfect companion is drawn to me.

9. I trust myself to make good choices in love and to attract not only my forever partner who is my best friend.

10. I release any past relationships and forgive myself and anyone involved and let go of any former relationships which no longer serve me. In doing so I have created a beautiful space for my perfect soulmate.

11. I feel a deep union with my loved one, I trust the Universe to bring us together in a beautiful way. I am open to love.

12. Write out your affirmations.

_____

_____

_____

_____

_____

_____

_____

_____

_____

_____

_____

_____

CHAPTER 3 MANIFESTING ABUNDANCE

Recommended Crystals

Citrine, Pyrite, Green Jade

Suggested Talisman

Dollar sign, keychain, symbolic necklace or ring. Your talisman can even be a picture of a desired vacation or a photo of your desire good. My key chain says "Thank you Father-mother God- For my home paid in full". You can even write out a check to yourself for the amount of money you desire.

Your talisman can be anything that represents your desire.

Money, Abundance & Things

A lot of people will say they want money, but what they actually want is the thing that money represents. If you want new computer, you can either manifest the money for the computer or start with the answer, a new computer.

Watch your thinking. Watch your words. Watch your energy.

Your first exercise in this section is to understand your relationship with money. Do this by sitting quietly with a dollar bill in your hand. As you hold the bill, have a conversation with yourself about money.

Write down, how you feel about money? Is it a happy relationship or are you resentful because there is never enough?

_____

_____

_____

_____

When did I begin to have an issue with money?

_____

_____

_____

_____

_____

How do I feel when I spend money? Do I feel joy and gratitude or concern if I use it, won't return?

_____

_____

_____

_____

_____

_____

Write down any negative or fear-based thoughts you have about money.

_____

_____

_____

_____

_____

_____

_____

_____

_____

Do I believe I don't have enough money?

_____

_____

_____

Do I focus on lack or abundance?

_____

Do I feel uncomfortable accepting a gift or compliment?

_____

How do I feel when I pay my bills, make my car payments, my mortgage or home payment?

_____

Do I spend my money with joy and appreciation or from a place of lack?

_____

Do I give and receive money with a sense of gratitude for the

good I have received?

_____

_____

_____

_____

_____

Visualizations

Sit with your feet squarely on the ground. Take deep yoga breaths to calm your body and bring your body into alignment with the abundance of the Universe.

As you close your eyes, imagine a beautiful tree before you. As you fully visualize this lush green tree, I want you to count the leaves. In less than a millimeter, you realize counting all the leaves is an impossible task. You realize the lesson not to count the leaves but to understand like the tree, all you need is already within you.

Shopping Mall Visualization

Shoppers are hurrying about with store bags; teenagers are running in and out of music stores and families are enjoying a meal at the food court.

You begin to walk past stores and take note of the items in store displays that you intend on purchasing soon but you continue on to a bank. Your bank.

When you arrive at the bank, you see a small welcome sign with your name on it. Several tellers smile as you walk in. You walk to the nearest representative. There is no waiting, no delay for you. As the cashier welcomes you and you share, you'd like to check your balance and make a withdrawal.

She turns her computer toward you and you smile at

the amount shown. Its more than you imagined. You tell, the cashier, you want to transfer to your earthly bank account. She efficiently transfers funds from your heavenly bank account to your local bank account. You are now assured you have all the funds you need. All your bills are paid in full with additional money in your account.

As the transfer is completed, the Universe immediately replenishes your account. You always have money you need when you need. Your Universal account overflows in financial abundance.

You feel an overwhelming sense of gratitude, for you know you are a beloved child of the Universe. As you align your energy with these feelings of financial abundance, prosperity and wealth, you speak your thanks.

This or something more now manifests for you.

Mini-Visualization

Throughout the day, when you are in a safe place, and not driving or operating a motorized vehicle, close your eyes for a mini-visualization.

In this mini-visualization, you see yourself standing on top of a small hill. The sun is shining on you. You feel the warmth and feel blessed.

As you watch the sky, beautiful blossoms fall toward you. Watch as the sky is filled with beautiful flower pedals.

Just as they reach you, the blossoms turn to dollar bills. You extend your arms for you realize this financial abundance is yours! All yours! There is abundance for all!

Stay in this moment, until you feel the abundance of all you need.

When the mini-visualization is over, say thank you Father-Mother-God. This or something greater now manifests in my life. And So, It Is.

Affirmations

1. I now accept love, health, harmony, and financial abundance in my life. I enjoy the flow of financial abundance in my life. I am worthy of an unending stream of financial abundance.

2. My world is filled with financial abundance. I am open, willing and grateful to I accept my good in all things.

3. I enjoy the flow of financial abundance in my life. I easily pay my bill with the knowledge that money is continuously flowing into my life. I am worthy of every good thing.

4. I am a money magnet. Everything I touch turns to gold.

5. I activate the Law of Attraction and money freely and effortless flows into my life.

6. I always have more money than I need. I spend my money wisely and know I have money to share, money to pay my bills and live debt free.

7.. I release any negative beliefs about money and accept I am a child of God, worthy of every good thing.

8. I now accept love, health, harmony, and financial abundance in my life. I enjoy the flow of financial abundance in my life.

9. I now give thanks for my new car (house, boat, etc.). I completely and fully trust the Universe to now create a new world filled with happiness, prosperity and security.

10. That which I conceive, I achieve. I open to financial abundance!

11. I joyfully pay my bills, knowing what money I send out, returns to me multiplied. Money is in a constant flow in my life.

Money needs to be in a constant state of flow. It's okay to add to your savings or hold onto it for a prosperous future; just don't hold onto it out of the fear that if you spend it, it won't return. Using your credit cards for abundance, does not count.

CHAPTER 5 CAREER, EMPLOYMENT

Recommended Crystals

Pyrite and Citrine for money and wealth.

Rose Quartz and Clear Quartz to assist you in communication.

Green Aventurine also helps to open the door for new opportunities.

Lapis lazuli promotes communication, stimulates self-expression and mental clarity.

Turquoise and Aquamarine to help you in organizing your thoughts, excellent for clarity and will help you communicate.

Blue Sapphire is another good crystal to help you support your throat chakra and communication skills.

Crystals for Balance and Calming Black Tourmaline Celestite. Fluorite and beautiful Tiger's Eye.

Suggested Talismans

` A key chain with dollar or money symbol, a 4-leaf clover or photo of a career that you now want to manifest.

I am going to divide this section into two parts. The first part is for those who are working but are wanting to improve their situation.

Part Two is for those who want to simply reinvent themselves. This life event has occurred through relocation, divorce, retirement or a desire to explore a new career.

I use this technique when working with people to bring clarity or find a new direction in their lives.

New Job
Questions

What do I hope to gain in a new position?

_____
_____
_____
_____
_____
_____
_____
_____

What benefits am I looking for in a new position? Higher salary, Insurance, education, gym memberships?

_____
_____
_____
_____

Visualize your office or work station.

_____
_____
_____
_____
_____

Visualize small details like coffee, snacks, a refrigerator or microwave in the break room?

_____
_____
_____
_____
_____

Is it important to you that your company has integrity and

supports community with events like food drives or having a toy donation box at the holidays?

_____

_____

_____

_____

_____

_____

How far close to home are you willing to drive? Or is your ideal job working at home in a remote position.?

_____

_____

_____

_____

_____

What are the prerequisites and skills you need for your new position?

_____

_____

_____

_____

_____

_____

Do you believe you are worthy of such a position?

_____

_____

_____

_____

_____

What do you envision your relationship with your supervisor and coworkers will be? See your supervisors supportive of you and value you.

_____

_____

_____

_____

_____

_____

While driving to an interview, reinforce your vision of getting this job, by thinking, this is the way I drive to work. I stop and get office here and this is my parking space as you part your car.

_____

_____

_____

_____

_____

Remember always affirm, this or something better is now yours, until you find the position you truly want.

Describe the perfect day for you and infuse as many happy details as possible. The Universe will take your vision and bring your image into manifestation.

Affirmations

1. I speak my word for a job close to home, where I am valued, and appreciated by coworkers and supervisors.

2. There is no delay in the diving plan for me. My desire to work, and be of service is my prayer answered.

3. I am grateful for the job offered to me. I give thanks my job pays more than I imagined.

4. I now give thanks as I manifest the perfect employment for me.

5. I am worthy of the fantastic job I desire. I am led to the right job, at the right salary, at the right location for the highest good of my experience.

6. I move forward in confidence and assurance that I have the

right job for me.

7. I am open experience my dream job with the salary I desire to easily support my lifestyle and my needs and the needs of my family.

8. Thank you, Father-Mother-God, for my new job now.

9. I trust the Universe to bring me and my new job together

10. I am fulfilled and grateful for my new job.

Finish by affirming, in faith, "This or something better now manifests for me. And So, It Is!"

A New Career or Reinventing Yourself

This is an exercise I recommend when I am working with someone who fits the above criteria.

First Write 10 Ten Things that you would love to do. Do not think of how you will accomplish this or that you are too old, young or any other label, I insist you have fun with this exercise!

Ten fields in which you would like to work it?

_____

_____

_____

_____

_____

_____

_____

_____

_____

_____

_____

_____

_____

_____

Next to each topic, write down 10 jobs or position you can find in the field that most appeals to you.

For example, you select a career working with animals. Write beside it 10 ways you could earn a living working with animals. Occupations can include but not limited to a veterinarian or veterinarian assistant, jobs at a local zoo, a dog trainer, dog walker, pet sitter or wildlife conservation officer, park ranger or educator, pet groomer, animal communicator or wildlife photographer.

Some of your careers may require education. If so, remember you are never too old to begin study in the field you want to find work in. In the meantime, volunteer at a local animal shelter or start as a dog walker business. Get moving into a career you would truly enjoy.

You may be a bit older than required to be a full-fledged astronaut but you are never too old to inspire children and adults with your fascination of space. So, without giving up your dream, look for careers in which you could live your aspiration. For instance, you could become a scientist, engineer or a tour guide at Kennedy Space Center or museum, become trained to work on a satellite or space ship, become a science fiction author, a teacher or librarian or assistant.

You have now selected a new career for yourself, write down the steps you need.to to accomplish that goal. Share it with your friends who will support you and brainstorm with you to make your new vocation a reality.

See yourself in your new role and allow the Universe to magically make it happen.

CHAPTER 7 HEAL
THE PLANET

Recommended Crystals

Brown Aragonite Herkimer Diamonds Smokey Quartz Fairy Amethyst

Suggested Talisman

Your talisman can be reusable water tumbler, coffee cup, a key ring with an earth, a stress ball or a beautiful picture of a beach or landscape.

Earth

It is our privilege, pleasure and responsibility to call this planet home.

I think everyone reading this book recognizes that our beautiful planet needs our prayers. For the air to the waters, precious animal species, our prayers can change our lives, our prayers can change the planet. Humans are the cause but we can also be the solution.

I urge everyone reading this book to create a personal action plan for this important issue.

Personal Action Plan for the Planet

Going forward, create a list of things you can do to help the planet. Things can include recycling, feeding wildlife in your area, donating to animal causes or thinking positive thoughts. You may wish to use reusable containers, conserve electricity, conserve water and as time allows, to volunteer for cleanups and animal care.

Send positive thoughts to the planet and universe and always show kindness.

My Action Plan

_____

_____

_____

_____

_____

_____

_____

_____

Visualizations

Sit with your feet squarely on the ground. Take deep yoga breaths to calm and bring your body into alignment with the earth energy.

As you close your eyes, you are aware of a deep and beautiful peace deep within you. You allow this blissful energy to fill every cell, every part of your body with love.

As this beautiful feeling grows within you, you feel as silverly glistening roots shoot out from your feet and extend downward into the earth where they wrap around a beautiful golden core. Feeling safe and secure, you see your energy flow back to your body.

As you return to the earth's surface, you open your mind's eye you find yourself in a deep green forest. You are standing in a small clearing with a canopy of trees above you. The air is cool to your skin, and feels comfortable, part of nature. You catch the soft fragrance of wildflowers in the air carried by a gentle wind that caresses your face. You are safe, sheltered and protected.

As you look about you, you watch as shimmering streams of golden light slip through the green canopy to the forest floor. With the light brightening the forest, you see a doe grazing on the path before you. She pauses to watch you then disappears into the woods. She knows you are here to help her and her kind.

Three small rabbits scamper in front of you and you are

suddenly aware of the sounds of birds chirping in the trees and the occasion dark flutter of a bird crossing through the light.

You notice a path is before you and you begin to walk down that trail. As you walk along, you see you are traveling next to a beautiful stream and flows around rocks. The water is so clear, you see fish darting in and about the water's edge. The water is sparkles at sunlight shimmers in the current. You are keenly aware of the fresh scent of the stream.

As you continue walking the forest gives way to tall grasses and you follow the path to a sandy dune. Reaching the top of the dune, you happily discover a long sandy beach.

You walk down to the beach and smell the heady scent of sea. In the distance, you watch as sea gulls glide across the top of white foamy waves. A small crab digs a hole into the sand and disappears into the sand. The sand feels crunching beneath your feet.

You walk to the water's edge and allow small waves to dance playfully around your feet. The water is warm and inviting and you walk into the sea. When it's up to your chest, you dive. In this realm you can swim and you enjoy the water world around you.

As you swim, you can feel all the negative thoughts, cares of the world, all concerns just float away from you. Dolphins join you and if you wish you can grab a fin or ride the back of them

As you return to shore, you stand and open your arms and let the sun bathe you with its warm golden rays.

In peace and in power, you allow your loving energy flow from you and expand, filling your world, this planet with beautiful healing light. The energy you send to the world eliminates pollution's, dissolves chemicals and plastics, you realize your power to make the oceans healthy again and teaming with fish.

Your energy cleans the land, the streams and rivers and restores the plane to health.

You envision world peace and so it is as you watch leaders

of countries come together. Children are fed, everyone is loved and the kindness in you is so powerful, the earth, is restored.

Allow yourself a moment to feel that which you have done this day and be grateful for this planet and your part in healing it.

Slowly, you open your eyes and are assured your visualization. Your word, your loving energy has transformed the earth into a more peaceful and beautiful place.

My personal manifestation for World Peace and Healing

_____
_____
_____
_____
_____
_____

Affirmations

1. Today more than ever before, I do my part to heal the planet. I recognize myself as an important part of this change. And so, it is.

2. I give thanks for my beautiful, healthy perfect planet.

3. As I speak my word for peace and goodwill to all men, women and children of this planet, my loving thoughts bring world harmony to all nations, to all people.

4. As I speak my word for clean streams and clean air, my loving energy spreads across the planet and makes the water pure and the planet whole and refreshed.

5. I give thanks for restoration and an abundance of wildlife.

6. Everytime I eat good food, drink water, I give thanks for my good and as I do so, my attitude of gratitude blesses the waters, renews the land and all who walk upon it.

7. At the core of my being, there is an infinite well of love. As I send this love, my love across the globe, my loving energy touches the heart and minds of every man, woman and child in this world.

8. My thoughts of a peaceful planet are answered. My thoughts

of health and abundance creates health and abundance of all, for all.

9. I now visualize my love and peace circulating the planet. Wars stop, children and animals are loved, this planet experiences a renaissance of life.

10. As I send out love to all the earth, all creatures great and small experience peace and a bounty of love and kindness.

Chapter 8 Conclusion

I hope you have enjoyed this Manifestation thru

Visualization and Affirmation and this workbook.

I wrote this book and workbook because I have successfully manifested many things in my life. I started my journey with my first money manifestation $25.00. Today, I can manifest a four-bedroom house or a car. The good news is you can too!

As I shared the secret to the Law of Attraction is in the details. Those details include aligning your energy with the Laws of Vibrations, Correspondence and feelings of worthiness and acceptance. All these laws must come into alignment and belief in order for your manifest dream to be achieved.

The elements in this book will only work, if you apply them.

Some of your manifestation will occur instantly. Others may will take a moment, it depends on you and aligning your energy and frequency.

As I close this book, I have included a recommended books and resources to expand on your journey along with a chapter on my book Reincarnation Journey of the Soul.

Again, thank you very much for reading my book. I appreciate it so much and would appreciated a kind review after you have read it.

Whatever you dream about, it can be yours if you claim it, believe it and align your energy with it. I will be in your front row clapping!

Jessica Wallace King
www.Clairoyant Jess.com

When I first learned of the Law of Attraction, the basic marching orders were, "what man can conceive, he will achieve" or simply told "to believe and say affirmations 100 times a day."

It wasn't until I fully embraced quadrium physics and The Akashic Records did I fully understand the importance of aligning the soul's energy with the desire to make the Law of Attraction successful.

If you would like a teacher and practitioner to assist you, I'd like to recommend Jessica Wallace King. Jess has developed a full class that offers individual consultation along with the information on how to align your energies with your manifestation goals.

Her course is based on the fundamentals of manifestation featured in this book. The first two classes are general in nature. Jess will help you identify blocks in your life and how to align your energy with your desire.

Once you complete the two very intensive hour-long class sessions, Jess will work with you individually through a one-on-one dynamic coaching session. Individual sessions are structured keep your manifestation goals private as well to overcome that which might be holding you back. If you require additional private coaching and counselling sessions, she will be delighted to work with you for as long as needed. One private counselling session is included in her class.

To take advantage of this extraordinary teacher, you can contact or register for her ongoing classes at her website, www.clairvoyantjess.com.
You are of course welcome to contact me through my website of www.LinnRandom.com.

Thank you again for investing in your dreams by purchasing my book, *Manifestation thru Visualization and Affirmation.*

I'd love and appreciate a kind review!

Please know, it is my goal to help you bring all your dreams into the manifest plane for your best and highest good come true, and so it is!

Recommended Reading

In addition to the books listed below, I recommend any and all books by Dr. Raymond Moody, Brian Weiss, and James Van Praagh.

I encourage you to continue your study and interest in past lives to understand there is no death, only life, after life, after life.

To understand karma and the need to rise above it through forgiveness and love and release.

Jack and Cornelia Addington - *Your Needs Met*

Aristotle – *Metaphysics*

Rhonda Byrne - *The Secret.*

Judy Hall - *The Crystal Bible*

Louise Hay - *You Can Heal Your Life*

Debbie Hardy - *Meditation Made Easy Using Crystals:*
Spirit of the Crystal Ray & Mastering the Art of Allowing

Napoleon Hill - *The Power of Positive Thinking*

Ernest Holmes -*Science of Mind*

Nick Ortner - *The Tapping Solution*

Eckhart Tolle - *The Power of Now: A Guide to Spiritual Enlightenment.*

Linn Random - *The Business Side of a Spiritual Practice*

Linn Random *Reincarnation Journey of the Soul*

Crystals Recommendation

Debbie Hardy
www.hardycrystalblessing.com

Linn Random

www.LinnRandom.com

www.Linn Random Author Page, Amazon.com

About the Author

Linn Random is a Religious Science practitioner with over 40 years' experience.

Linn also runs her own spiritual practice, Sacred Angel Therapy. She is a certified Angelic Life Coach, Fairyologist, and is an Akashic Record Reader, Certified Angelic Life Coach, Oracle Card Reader, and is Certified Crystal Healing.

Linn Random is a marketing and communications specialist with a comprehensive background in domestic and international marketing.

Her experience includes all aspects of Public Relations campaign and strategy, including Copy Writing, Event Planning, Media Kits and Public Relations.

When she first retired, she was the National Director of an International Marketing firm, and in the mid-1990s, she was Executive Vice-President of a major Internet Company and became involved in all aspects of marketing and promotion on the world wide web.

Romantic Suspense Novels

Linn Random has loved romantic suspense since she watched Snow White run from the woodcutter's ax into the arms of a handsome Prince.

Her Romance Novels offer readers spine-tingling suspense, action-packed excitement, and characters that sparkle with intensity and emotion. Reviews state over and over that her novels are fresh, with multilayered plots.

Linn Random has been a frequent guest speaker at groups such as Sisters in Crime, numerous chapters of the Romance Writers of America, the Florida Writers Association, the Mystery Writers of America's Sleuthfest, and has taught online classes.

Linn lives in Central Florida with her husband and two dogs, Wally, and Bae.

For more information about Linn, visit

www.LinnRandom.com

Reincarnation Journey of the Soul (c) Excerpt

By Linn Random

Chapter 1
World View of Reincarnation

The word Reincarnation comes from the Latin word "to be made flesh again".

Reincarnation is the belief that after the body dies, we return to the spirit realm to be reunited with our loved ones before reincarnating into a new life and different body. Reincarnation is the belief in life after life after life.

There are certain religions, such as Hinduism and Buddhism, that hold this tenant as a cornerstone of their faith.

The early Christian church believed in reincarnation until the Council of Nicaea in 325 A.D. At the time, Christianity was a fledging and very fragile new religion. To stem the quarrels and in-fighting amongst the various factions, the Roman Emperor Constantine gathered the church leaders and formed an ecumenical council known as the First Council of Nicaea.

The objective of the council was to formulate a common core of beliefs. After much debate, the Holy Fathers set forth a statement of faith known as the Apostles' Creed. They chose the holy days for Christian observances and established canon law.

They also removed any reference to reincarnation which at that time was a common belief held by Christians.

The Second Council of Nicaea met in 553 A.D. This time, the Council proclaimed that the belief in reincarnation was heresy and punishable by death.

No reason was ever presented as to why the belief in reincarnation was removed. One could surmise that the church would have greater control over the people and their money. If the populace believed in reincarnation, they wouldn't feel the need to tithe the church or pay for extra services such as buying their way out of purgatory or hell. If people understood karma carried its own consequences, they would not need a confessional and would think twice before harming one another.

The Council of Nicaea also removed seven books from the Bible that conflicted with their newly pressed tenets and doctrines. The books that were eliminated contained information about Jesus' childhood, his siblings, reincarnation, and spiritual truths taught in the first few centuries of Christianity. Four scriptures on reincarnation remained in the New Testament.

The first appearance of reincarnation occurred when Jesus and his disciples came upon a blind man. They asked Jesus, "Rabbi, who sinned, this man or his parents, that he was born blind?"

His disciples were asking if the man was born blind due to his own actions in a previous life or was, he born blind because of his parent's deeds or actions. KJV, John 9:1-3.

In King James Version, Luke 9:20, Jesus asked his disciples, "Whom do the people say I am?"

Jesus asked because it was prophesized in KJV, Malachi 4:5 that God would send a messenger to prepare the way before the Messiah's return.

The disciples answered. "Some say that thou art John the Baptist, some, Elias; and others, Jeremias, or one of the prophets.'" KJV Matthew 16:13-19.

The disciples shared that many believed Jesus to be the reincarnation of the Prophet Elijah or Jeremiah. KJV, John 1:21

Jesus answered them by saying. "But I say unto you, that Elijah is come already, and they knew him not." Matthew 17:12, KJV. Jesus was referring to John the Baptist.

I want to interject that we live in a world of invisible and universal laws. These laws, work for everyone without exception. Two examples of these universal laws are the Law of Gravity and the Law of Centrifugal Force. Both laws work equally for everyone. Therefore, one must conclude, if reincarnation works for one, it must work for all.

In another instance, Jesus and the disciples, came upon a Pharisees, named Nicodemus. The disciples asked, "How can a man be born when he is old? Can he enter the second time into his mother's womb, and be born?" John 3:3 New American Standard Bible.

Jesus replied, "Truly, truly, I tell you, no one can see the kingdom of God unless he is born again."

Lastly, I point to the statement that Jesus said, "In my Father's house are many rooms; if it were not so I would have told you. I am going to prepare a place for you." John 14:2, KJV.

Jesus was not speaking of literal mansions. He was speaking of our physical bodies which are referred to as the temples of our souls. 1st Corinthians 6:19.

Reincarnation was not a new concept during the time of Christ, nor did it develop in India as many people believe.

`   References to reincarnation can be found in Norse legends and Germanic paganism.

Reincarnation appeared in Greek texts around 700 B.C. and plays a central role in Buddhism and Hinduism. It also surfaces in Jainism and Sikhism, two faiths that grew out of Hinduism.

The Yoruba and Edo Tribes of western Africa once believed they would be reborn into the same families as their own future descendants. The Zulu people once held the belief that a person's can be reborn as human or as different animals.

The Inuit populations that inhabit the Arctic regions of Greenland, Canada and Alaska also believe they can be reborn as humans or animals. They believed that an individual's incarnation depends on the way he or she lived and treated others.

I believe that we do not incarnate from an intellectually higher species to a one of lesser intelligence. I do believe the choice to return is ours and our decision to return is based on the lessons we choose to undertake.

In the last century, the concept of reincarnation was re-introduced to the western world by the transcendentalism movement that grew in the late 1820s and 1830s in the eastern United States.

In the 1930s the concept of reincarnation was again introduced to the world-by-world renowned psychic Edgar Cayce, known as The Sleeping Prophet.

The interest in reincarnation was jump-started in recent times through the teachings and books by Betty J. Eadie, Dr. Brian Weiss, Dick Sutphen and other New Age philosophers and religious leaders.

Today approximately 30 million Americans believe in reincarnation. More than half of the world's population shares this belief. Many people believe that number is actually higher.

I find no conflict with the teaching of Jesus or other religious leaders who advise mankind to be tolerant, kind to others with the warning that what you send out comes back multiplied.

.   To understand this philosophy is to understand how karma holds us responsible for our lives and how we teach others.

We come here, to this earth plane, to balance our karma, understand the lessons of life, love and forgiveness with the ultimate goal of unification with God.

We return to new cycles of life after life after life.

CORD CUTTING ©
People, Past Lives, Events

By Linn Random

Chapter 1 What is Cord Cutting?

Etheric cords are strands of energy that bind us to people, places, and things. Etherical cords bind us to those we love and those who love us.

We can feel these cords tugging and pulling at us when we sense a loved one is in need. We sometimes sense the moment before a friend calls, and we answer our phones and say, "I was just thinking about you."

A parent can sense her child in distress from hundreds of miles away. Many people describe waking at an odd hour during the night, thinking of a friend or relative only to discover the following day, their dear one had passed away at that exact time.

Etherical Cords also bind us to past experiences, situations, and people. We want to keep the beautiful, loving cords; the ones that bind us to those we love and who love us. These cords also connect us to beautiful memories that warm our hearts.

We also have cords that bind us to negative experiences and toxic relationships. Our bodies are the barometers of our souls and warn us against danger if only we'd listen.

I see etherical cords as fine, shimmering, silvery, magical tubing that glitters and sparkles between us and those we love.

Etherical cords can stretch back centuries. We feel a connection when we meet strangers. We are so instantly comfortable with these people; it seems we have known them all our lives.

The French term déjà vu means "already seen." We are also bound to places by etherical cords. Many first-time visitors to battlefields or streets share these places that seem so instantly familiar to them. If you have had such a déjà vu experience, you may have remarked to friends at the time, "I feel as though I have been here before." Perhaps you have.

Etherical Cords can also bind us to traumatic experiences.

For instance, the backfire of a car can instantly transport a veteran to a combat theater where they fought decades ago.

Post-traumatic stress disorder is commonly associated with wartime experiences. However, it can include children who witnessed or were an unwilling participant in abuse, or those who experienced natural disasters.

Have you ever met anyone who is inherently afraid of water, fire, heights or bees, specific animals or reptiles? Many people who have these phobias do not have a childhood link or memory to any experience in their phobias which are both real and sometimes terrifying. These fears may have come from life lived centuries ago, one in which an etherical cord still connects you.

I may very well be the only person in America who became unnerved at the sight of a Viking longboat. It's okay to laugh, I do, but I also have a clear and distinct memory of Vikings attacking an abbey where I lived in 793 AD.

I endured a horrific death in that lifetime, though I had no recall of it until that moment. Yet, it was there, and I was bound to it by an etherical cord. That particular memory lay hidden in the dark recesses of my soul's memory until a television documentary triggered it.

That night, my body shook, my throat went dry, and I was stricken in fear. I experienced uncontrollable heart palpations, so much so, I had to get up and leave the room to catch my breath.

A few days later, in past-life regression, I saw my death on the steps of a monastery at the hands of a Viking berserker. I understood why the image was so terrifying to me. With the source identified, I cut the etherical cord that bound me to my experience.

Perhaps the frightening visions conjured in dreams are not nightmares but memories.

Children's nightmares may be born from past life when their boogie man was real.

If you have the same recurring nightmare, you may benefit from identifying the cause and removing it from your experience through a cord-cutting.

Whether in this lifetime or a previous life, we sometimes hold onto memories that are so deep, we can no longer recall a single incident that binds us to these memories and experiences.

Once, when I was working with a beautiful young woman, I could sense a past relationship she was holding onto. It was blocking her from experiencing the loving relationship she now longed for. I could clearly see and sense she was still bound by the solid etherical cord she had created with her former lover.

"Do you think of that him more than three times a week?" I asked, already anticipating her answer.

She laughed. "I think of him three times an hour."

I worked with her, and together we successfully cut the cord to this unhealthy relationship. As if on cue, a wonderful man appeared. Today, she is happily married and enjoys life in a loving, supportive relationship

Most Etherical Cords are not so easily identifiable.

Etherical Cords can stretch to past lives where we made vows of poverty or chastity. We spoke our oaths with such deep sincerity, they are still attached to us and twist and distort their way throughout current finances and relationships.

I have worked with clients who, despite their best efforts to climb out of debt, were simply unsuccessful. At first glance, they seemed to be doing all the right things to improve their finances, but there was something illusive, hiding in the shadows, that kept them from experiencing the success they deserved.

Unhealthy cords manifest in feelings of depression, melancholy, obsessive thoughts, and self-sabotaging behavior. These dysfunctional cords can twist and tangle people in unhealthy eating or drinking patterns. This type of etherical cord may be a carryover from a time when we experienced starvation or famine.

Some individuals have an instant addiction and connection to drugs or alcohol. Their connection may not come from a physical weakness or their bodies' predisposition to drugs and alcohol, but these addictions can be traced back to when they abused substances. That's why a drugged state is so familiar to them and feels so natural. They lived it before, and they know the dance steps to this macabre tune.

If any of these words or experiences resonate within you, a cord may need to be cut. The act of cutting a cord does not have to be a complicated ceremony. In fact, it can be very simple and take only a few minutes.

A single cord-cutting may suffice for most unhealthy etherical cords. However, some cords are older, stronger, tougher, and are so entwined with your psyche that they may reform and regrow. More than one cord cutting will be required if this is ever the case.

At the end of each chapter, you will find a Cord Cutting that will be relative to the chapter subject.

I work with Angels, so when I need to cord cut, I call on Archangel Michael and ask him to use his fiery sword to sever my ties to any person, place, or thing that does not serve me. After a cord-cutting, I always ask Archangel Raphael to salve the wound with his green healing light to complete the healing.

There are many types of cord-cutting techniques on the internet. Find one that works for you.

Sample Cord Cutting: Toxic Relationships

"I call on Archangel Michael to sever any cords created that bind me to negative experiences or emotions. I release any fears, doubts, feelings of unworthiness, self-denial, self-punishment, or any self-sabotaging behavior. I am free of any karmic debt or people in my life that cause me pain or suffering. I release all vows that no longer serve me. Going forward, I strengthen my cords of love to those who love me and whom I love. I awaken the ancient wisdom within me. I am now open to a beautiful new life filled with more love, joy, health, and abundance than I have"

Printed in Great Britain
by Amazon

43228406R00089